CAMBRIDGE PRIMARY
English

Activity Book

Gill Budgell and Kate Ruttle

CAMBRIDGE
UNIVERSITY PRESS

University Printing House, Cambridge CB2 8BS, United Kingdom

One Liberty Plaza, 20th Floor, New York, NY 10006, USA

477 Williamstown Road, Port Melbourne, VIC 3207, Australia

4843/24, 2nd Floor, Ansari Road, Daryaganj, Delhi – 110002, India

79 Anson Road, #06-04/06, Singapore 079906

Cambridge University Press is part of the University of Cambridge.

It furthers the University's mission by disseminating knowledge in the pursuit of education, learning and research at the highest international levels of excellence.

Information on this title: education.cambridge.org

© Cambridge University Press 2015

This publication is in copyright. Subject to statutory exception and to the provisions of relevant collective licensing agreements, no reproduction of any part may take place without the written permission of Cambridge University Press.

First published 2015
20 19

Printed in India by Repro India Ltd.

A catalogue record for this publication is available from the British Library

ISBN 978-1-107-69112-4 Activity Book

Cambridge University Press has no responsibility for the persistence or accuracy of URLs for external or third-party internet websites referred to in this publication, and does not guarantee that any content on such websites is, or will remain, accurate or appropriate.

Contents

1 Stories about things we know   4

2 How to write instructions   18

3 Rhymes about places and people we know   30

4 Tales from around the world   37

5 What is my house made of?   52

6 Poems by famous poets   68

7 Stories by famous writers   74

8 Things under the sea   90

9 All kinds of creatures   104

1 Stories about things we know

1 All about Sophie

A Write a fact file for two friends or people in your family. Ask them the questions and fill in the chart.

Name		
Age		
Birthday		
Family		
Personality		
Likes to wear		
Likes		
Wants to be		

Tip

Remember to ask a question using the **wh** question words:
What is your name?
How old are you? (*Miss this question out for a grown-up.*)
When is your birthday?
Who is in your family? *or* **How** many people are in your family?
How would you describe your personality?
What do you like to wear?
What do you like?
What do you want to be?

2 Reading and understanding A Bad Back

A Find these words in this part of the story and (circle) them.

Sound **ai**	Sound **ee**	Sound **igh**	Sound **oa**	Sound **ue**
they	peered	white	Sophie	blue
lay	peeped	in<u>side</u>	yell<u>ow</u>	through
made	ceiling	sighed	shad<u>ow</u>y	gloomily

A Bad Back by Dick King-Smith

Sophie was walking round the garden, wearing a pair of her mother's very old sunglasses. They were very dark glasses with a white frame. They made Sophie look like a panda. They made pink flowers look red and yellow flowers look golden and cabbages look blue.

Sophie walked along the path that ran along the front of the house and peered in through the dining-room window. Inside, everything looked very dark. But whatever in the world was that long shadowy thing lying on the floor?

In the dining room Sophie's father lay flat on the hard wood-block floor, his arms by his sides, and stared gloomily at the ceiling.

Sophie peeped round the door.

"Daddy?" she said.

"Yes."

"Are you all right?"

"No."

"What's the matter?"

"My back hurts."

"I'm not surprised," said Sophie. "Lying on that hard old floor. If you wanted to have a rest, why didn't you go to bed?"

Sophie's father sighed.

Session 2 Reading and understanding *A Bad Back*   5

3 Retelling and acting *A Bad Back*

A Use the pictures to retell the story to a friend or someone in your family. Draw a new ending for the story in the empty boxes.

B If this were your story ...

1 What would you call the main character?
   _____

2 Where would you set the story?
   _____

3 Who else would be in your story?
   _____

Unit 1 Stories about things we know

4 All about Mums

A Write the missing words. Then re-read the poem to check that it sounds right.

Use these words. You can use them more than once.

don't   won't   your
you   why   what

The Things Mums Say

Wake up!

Get up!

Out of bed!

Mind _____ feet!

Mind _____ head!

_____ run around.

_____ be late.

Look at _____ room!

_____ a state!

Put all _____ stuff away now, please.

_____ can I never find my keys?

Close _____ mouth and eat _____ food.

Look at that!

_____ stare, it's rude.

Elbows OFF the table, please.

Money doesn't grow on trees.

I _____ tell _____ again ...

Did _____ hear what I said?

I _____ tell you again.

It's time for bed.

Michaela Morgan

Session 4 All about Mums 7

5 Getting you to do something

A Sort these words from the story *Eat Your Peas*.

> like   even   again   say   Daisy   peas
> sighs   buy   green   bike   plate   stay

Write words with the **ai** sound. One has been done for you.

pay

Write words with the **ee** sound. One has been done for you.

tea

Write words with the **igh** sound. One has been done for you.

my

Unit 1 Stories about things we know

B Draw something you don't like to eat on this plate.

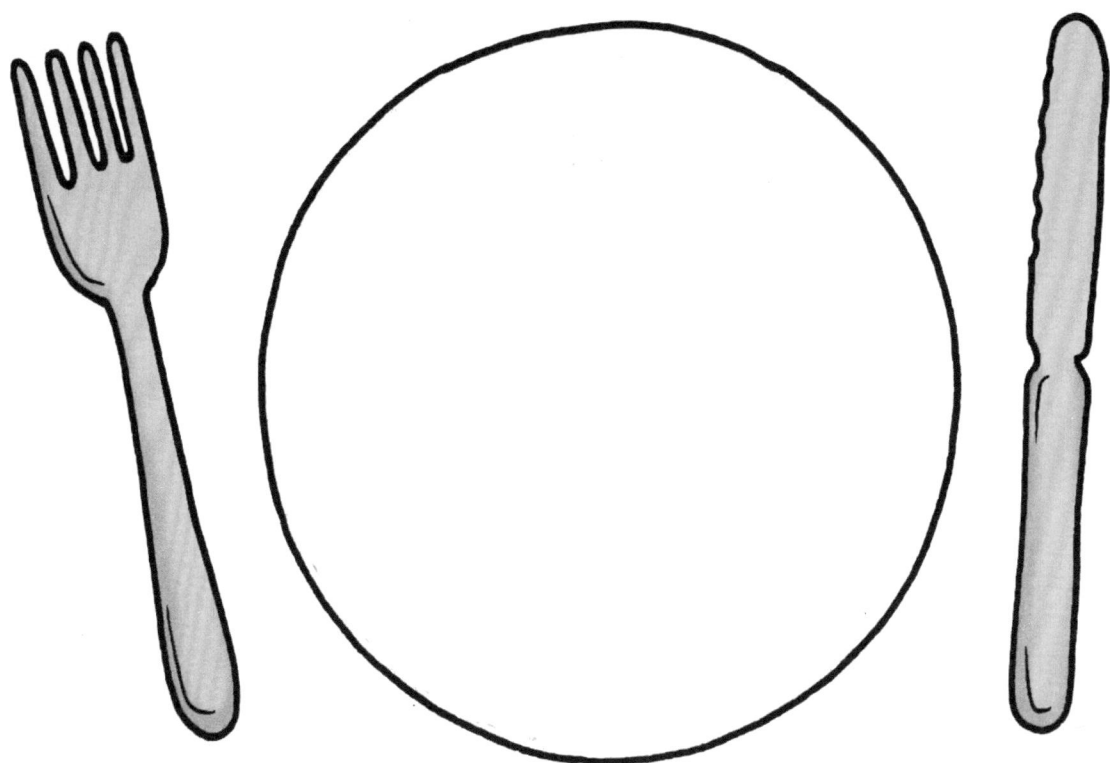

6 Checking *Eat Your Peas*

A Finish these sentences with your own ideas.

1 If you eat your apple, you never have to _____

2 If you eat your lunch, I'll buy you _____

3 If you drink your water, you can have _____

7 Exploring and writing

A Pretend you are a mum or dad. Finish the chart to show what **you** would promise your child to make them eat peas.

Try to make the ideas get bigger and better each time. They can be silly things!

You can draw or write the words.

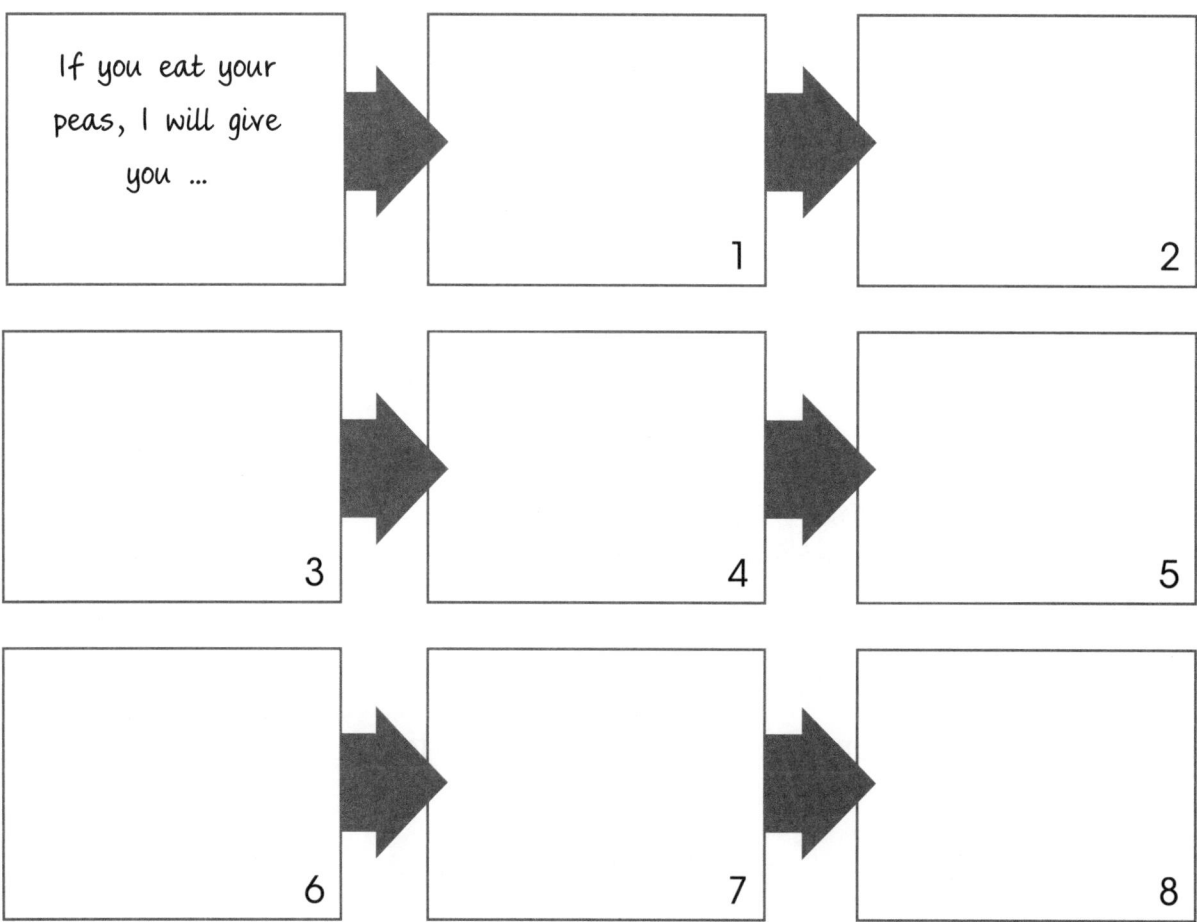

B Make a list of three things you do not like to do.

1 _____

2 _____

3 _____

Unit 1 Stories about things we know

8 Bunny Money

A Read this part of the story *Bunny Money* by Rosemary Wells.

> "Here's an idea!" said Rosalinda. "Bluebird earrings are four notes. Gift wrap is free."

The earrings would be packed in a small box. Draw gift wrapping on the box so it looks like a special gift. You may use some of these ideas:

B What gift would you choose for someone in your family?

_____

9 Checking and understanding *Bunny Money*

 Look at the things in the shop window.

The bunny money you have is 15 notes.

Choose what you will buy.

Write and draw what you buy.

_____

_____

_____

How much did you spend? _____

Who will you give the things to?

_____

Unit 1 Stories about things we know

10 Characters and settings

A Draw the faces of the characters in the story *Bunny Money*.

Write each character's name.

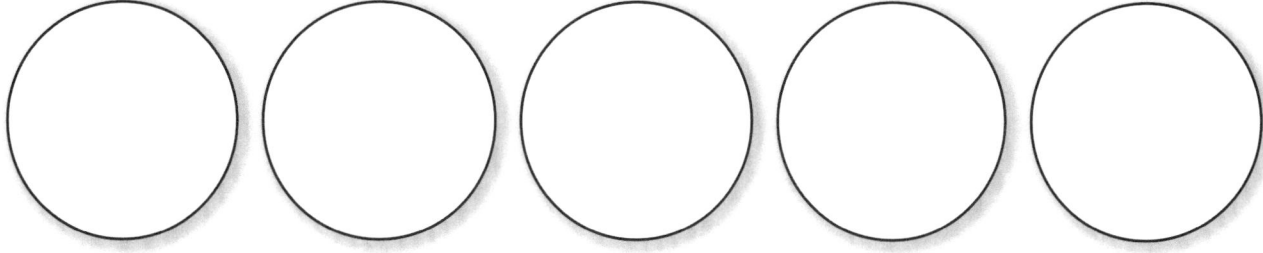

_____   _____   _____   _____   _____

B Circle all the words in the text that tell you about a setting. One is done for you.

1 Ruby took one note from her wallet to pay for the bus fare. (The bus) stopped at Rosalinda's Gift Shop.  In the window was a music box with skating ballerinas.	2 Next door was Candi's Corner and they sold sweets that were like teeth. 
3 Ruby had to take Max to the launderette. They spent three notes. 	4 "Hungry!" said Max. It was lunchtime. Max finished off a peanut butter sandwich, two coconut cupcakes, and a banana milkshake. Lunch cost four notes. 

11 Story sequence

A Make up new endings to these two parts of the story.

1

They walked all the way back to Rosalinda's Gift Shop … → "I'd like to buy the music box with skating ballerinas for Grandma's birthday," Ruby said to Rosalinda. "It's one hundred notes," said Rosalinda → Ruby looked in her wallet … ?

_____

_____

_____

2

"Thirsty!" said Max. "You may buy a very, very small lemonade, Max," said Ruby. → "Hungry!" said Max. It was lunchtime. → Max finished off … ?

_____

_____

_____

14 Unit 1 Stories about things we know

12 Changing the story

A Look at the picture. Write three questions that Max could ask to Candi, who works in the shop.

1 _____

2 _____

3 _____

B Draw your own money.

Will it be worth 1, 5, 10 or 100?

Unit review

A Make a honeycomb of your favourite words from this unit. Add extra bits to the honeycomb if you need to.

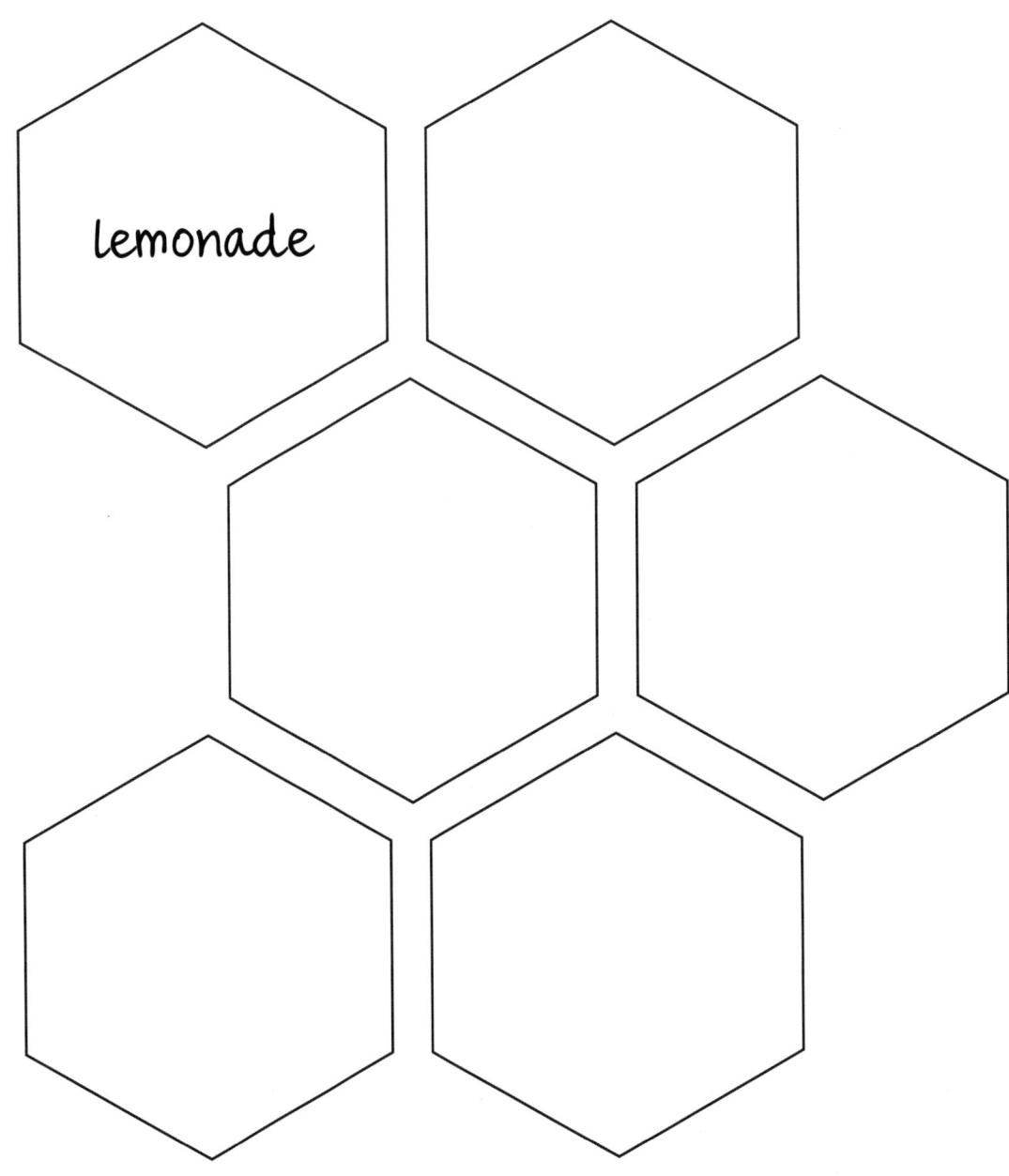

B Make a honeycomb of words from this unit that you need to practise writing. Add extra bits to the honeycomb if you need to.

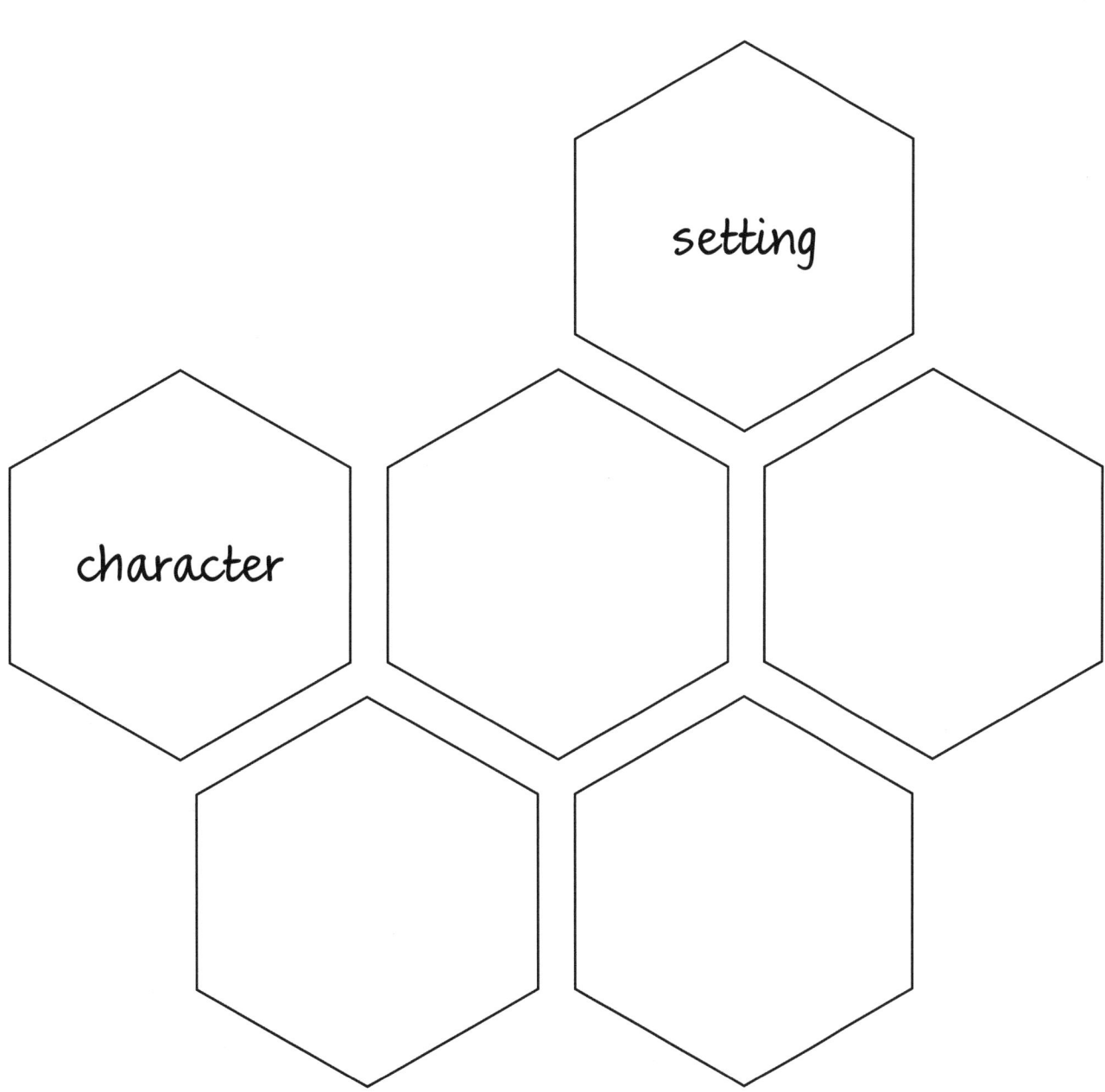

Unit review

2 How to write instructions

1 What do you know about instructions?

A Look at these instructions.

- What is each instruction telling you to do or not to do?
- Write a sentence about each.

Tip

Remember to use a capital letter at the beginning and a full stop or an exclamation mark at the end of your instructions. You may want to use *and* to join two parts of a sentence together.

1 ───────────────────────────────

2 ───────────────────────────────

3 ───────────────────────────────

4 ───────────────────────────────

B Write three Top Tips for helping someone to work well with a partner.

───────────────────────────────

───────────────────────────────

───────────────────────────────

2 How to be a scientist

A How many times can you find these words in the text?

- science _____
- scientist(s) _____
- experiment(s) _____

Circle them all as quickly as you can.

What do scientists do?

Scientists learn about the world around us by doing experiments.

What is an experiment?

An experiment is when you try to do something to find out what happens. You usually need to follow instructions.

Can I be a scientist?

Yes! You can learn about science. You can follow instructions to do some experiments just like a scientist!

B Read all of the words in the box. In each line, there is **one** word that does **not** have the sound **ai** as in *day*. Cross the word out.

make	put	say	wait	grey
they	bake	aim	may	look
play	main	eight	sort	take
apron	shake	read	wait	spray

The words have the same sound but different spellings.

3 Tips and rules

A Read the instructions about how to be a scientist.

Underline each instruction verb that tells you what to do or not to do. Look out! Sometimes there is more than one in a sentence.

How to be a scientist

Basic rules and instructions

- <u>Read</u> the experiment so you understand it.
- <u>Be</u> sure! <u>Check</u> with a grown-up if you do <u>not</u> understand any special science words.
- <u>Check</u> you have all the equipment (things you need) and get it ready.

Do you need to put on something to keep your clothes clean?

- Be safe! Check with a grown-up before you begin and ask for help with any tricky bits.

Do you need special goggles to keep your eyes safe?

- Wash your hands when you've finished. Never put your hands in your mouth or eat anything you find.
- Never play with heat or cleaning chemicals.
- Keep a notebook handy so you can draw or write up what happens. You can begin to make up your own experiments too.
- Always tidy up afterwards.

Remember to use a question mark.

B Write three questions about the instructions above.

For example: What should you never play with?
Ask friends or family to answer your questions. Test them!

1 _____

2 _____

3 _____

Unit 2 How to write instructions

4 How to blow bubbles

A Add **seven** full stops to this text. Write a capital letter after putting in each full stop. The first one has been done for you.

How to blow bubbles is an instructional text. It tells you about how you can blow bubbles each sentence adds new information to what you knew before so you have to read the text in order the text is in a chart and uses instruction verbs it has numbers and arrows to help you to understand the writing it makes the instructions clear but more fun too you should read the text so you know how to blow bubbles

B Answer these questions about the text in A.

1 Tick (✓) the features the writer found in the text:

☐ It tells you *how* to do something.

☐ The instructions are numbered.

☐ It has instruction verbs telling you what to do.

☐ It has headings, pictures and a chart.

2 Why did the writer like the chart? _____

_____

_____

5 Spotting extra information

A Add the missing words to these instructions.

These words tell you what to do in the right order.

| Secondly | Next | Then | Finally | First |

_____ make sure you have all your equipment.

_____ pour some water into a bowl.

_____ add some cooking oil.

_____ add some washing-up liquid.

_____ stir the water.

B Read all of the words. In each line, there is **one** word that does **not** have the sound **igh** as in *my*. Cross the word out.

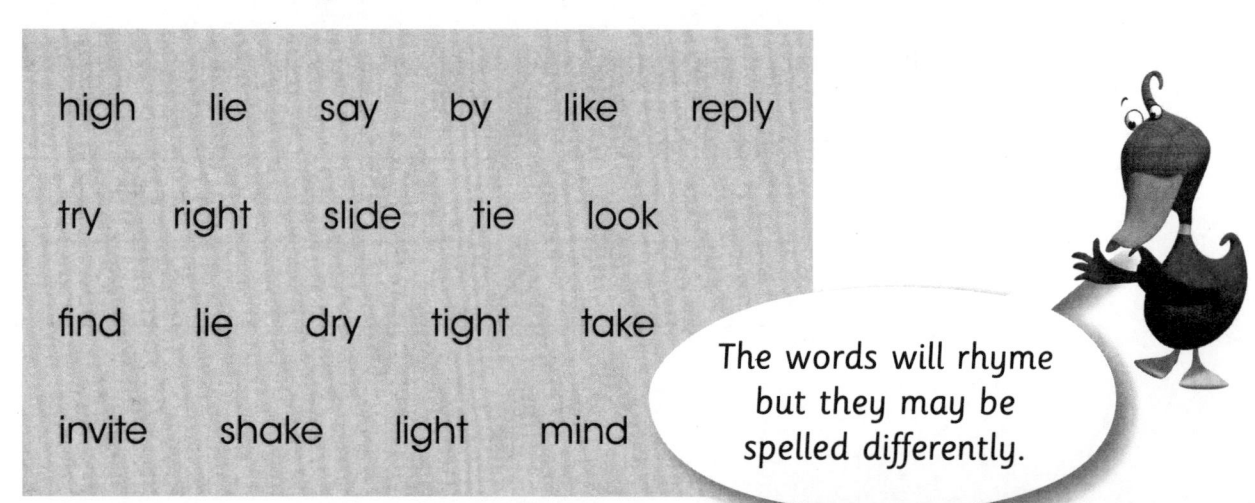

high	lie	say	by	like	reply
try	right	slide	tie	look
find	lie	dry	tight	take
invite	shake	light	mind

The words will rhyme but they may be spelled differently.

6 Sequence words

A Write *and* or *but* to join the sentences.

Make other punctuation changes. One is done for you.

1 You need a bowl. You need a jug of water.

   <u>You need a bowl and you need a jug of water.</u>

2 You need oil. You need some washing-up liquid.

   _____

3 You need a spoon. You do not need a fork.

   _____

4 Check your equipment. Pour some water into the bowl.

   _____

5 Add some cooking oil. Add some washing-up liquid.

   _____

6 You add some washing-up liquid. Only add a few drops.

   _____

B Count the syllables (or claps) in each word.

Write the number in the box.

spoon	water	jug	cooking
☐	☐	☐	☐
instruction	liquid	scientist	oily
☐	☐	☐	☐

7 Writing lists

A Look at each picture. Say what it is about.
Tick (✓) the best heading.

1

How to grow seeds ☐

How to eat beans ☐

2

How to make a hand puppet ☐

How to make a shadow ☐

3

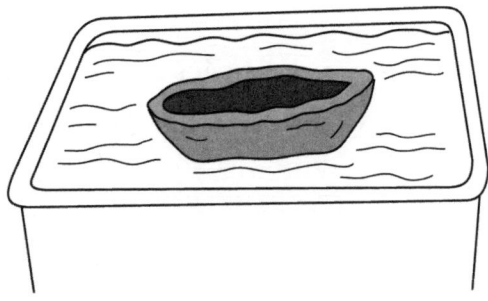

How to make a boat that floats ☐

How to play in sand ☐

4

How to make dirty coins shiny ☐

How to save pocket money ☐

B Read these **ere** words. Write a rhyming word with a different spelling.

here   where   there   were

_____   _____   _____   _____

Unit 2 How to write instructions

8 The correct order

A Write three tips for someone who has to speak about a project in class. Write a heading first.

How _____

B Draw 😊 or ☹ to show how well you speak out in class. ☐

How could you improve?

_____

_____

_____

Session 8 The correct order 25

9 Making notes

A Some children did an experiment called 'How to catch rain'.

They made a rain catcher and put it outside.

They checked it each day and made notes.

Here are their notes. Look at them and write a sentence for two of the days saying what the scientists saw.

How much rain?	Monday	Tuesday	Wednesday	Thursday	Friday
morning	Hot and sunny	No rain	Little rain	More rain 1.5 cm	Cloudy but no rain
afternoon	Quick shower 1 cm	Hot and sunny	More rain 1 cm	Heavy rain 3 cm	Sunny

1 On _____ day _____

_____

2 On _____ day _____

_____

B Look at these words.

said   old   house   about   your   there

Write each of the words inside its shape.

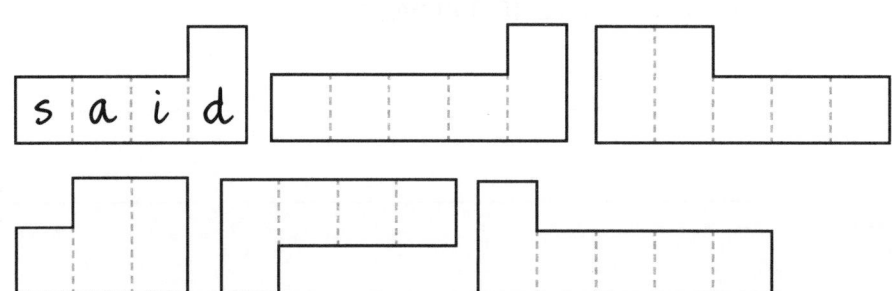

Unit 2 How to write instructions

10 Change it

A Fill in the gaps. The words in the box will help you.

> Write   about   again   stalks   see   how   blue   into   grown-up

How plants absorb water.

1 (Choose) three _____ of celery.

2 Ask a _____ to help you cut about 2 cm off the bottom of each celery stalk.

3 Pour water in to the glass jar. Fill it up to _____ half way.

4 Drop 3–4 drops of _____ dye into the jar.

5 Put the celery _____ the coloured water in the jar. Stir with the celery.

6 _____ down what you think will happen.

7 Leave overnight and check. Write what you _____ .

8 Leave overnight _____ and check. Write again what you see.

9 Check the bottom of the stalks. Write what you see.

10 Write what you found out about _____ plants absorb water.

B Circle all the verbs in the text that tell you what to do. One is done for you.

11 Check your understanding

A Use this chart to ask friends or family about this experiment.

	Test 1 Yellow dye in water	Test 2 Red dye in water
• Write the names of three people below. • Explain the experiment to them. • Ask: what do you think will happen to the white flower in each test? • Write what they say under each picture.		
1		
2		
3		

B Do you think they are right or wrong? Tick (✓) if right and write a cross (✗) if wrong.

Unit 2 How to write instructions

12 Improving instructions

A Find the pairs. Draw lines between pairs of words that mean the same.

Unit review

A Write a new word beginning with each letter of the word instruction.
It can be any word you know how to spell.

- i   _in_
- n   _no_
- s   _____
- t   _____
- r   _____
- u   _____
- c   _____
- t   _____
- i   _____
- o   _____
- n   _____

Unit review 29

3 Rhymes about places and people we know

1 Families

A Draw your family. Label who they are: mum, dad, brother, sister, cousin, aunty, uncle, grandma and grandad.

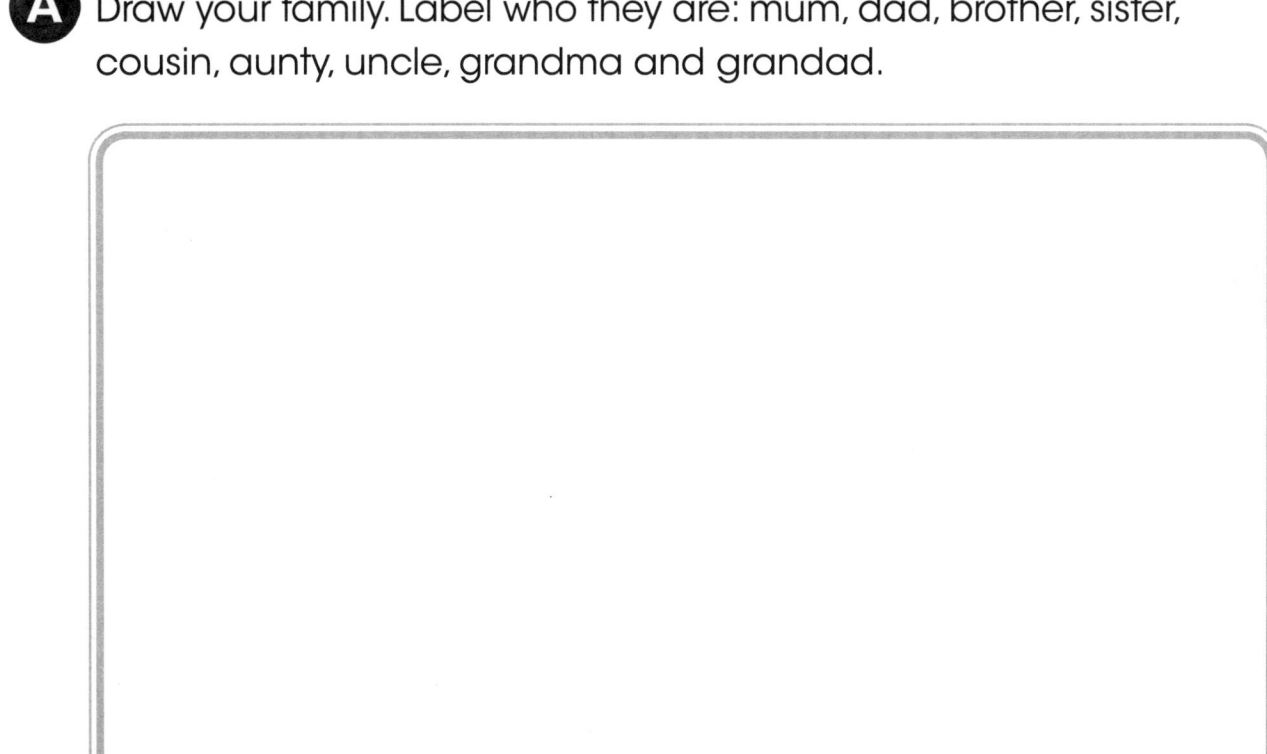

B Write questions that you think will get the answer, No!

1 Write a question for a Mummy or for an older person to answer.

_____

2 Write a question for a Daddy or for an older person to answer.

_____

3 Write a question for your teddy (or whatever toy is your favourite).

_____

2 Brothers and sisters

A Read the poem *Younger Brother*.

Write a list of the things he likes to collect.

There are 15 things.

Younger Brother

He collects bottle tops,
Toilet roll holders,
Dead insects,
Bits of rock and stones
Of interesting shapes and colours,
Half-made models,
Stickers, badges, pencils,
Feathers, germinating seeds,
Used socks (under the bed),
Broken saucers that he
never mends,
Torch batteries, glass marbles,
Oh – and friends.

Trevor Millum

B Write the missing double letters from the words below.

tt   **ll**   **ss**

Then write in the box how many syllables there are in each word.

co ___ ect ☐   bo ___ le ☐   ro ___ ☐

ba ___ eries ☐   gla ___ ☐   sy ___ able ☐

Session 2 Brothers and sisters

3 Family eating

 Match each name to the rhyming word for the food he or she likes.

Write each word if you can.

Underline any words that have double letters.

 Louise

_____

 Trish

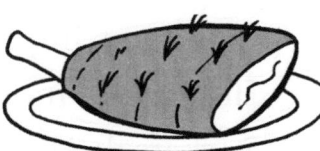
_____

 Pips

_____

 Pam

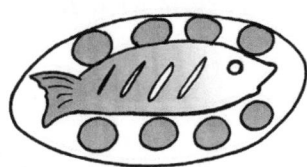
_____

 Greg

_____

 Kelly

_____

B Write two friends' names. Write a food that rhymes with each name.

_____   _____

_____   _____

C What do you notice about the first letter of all the names?

_____

Write the full alphabet A–Z in capital letters here.

A _____

_____

_____

4 Good manners

A Pretend that a friend of yours is going to tea with Aunty Mabel.

Write three tips about how to behave that begin with *DON'T* ...

1 _____

2 _____

3 _____

B Write three tips about how to behave that begin with *DO* ...

1 _____

2 _____

3 _____

5 Shopping

 A Label these shoes.

Use these words to help you.

> bow   heel   laces   sole   buckle   flashing light

Shoes for a party   **Shoes for sport**

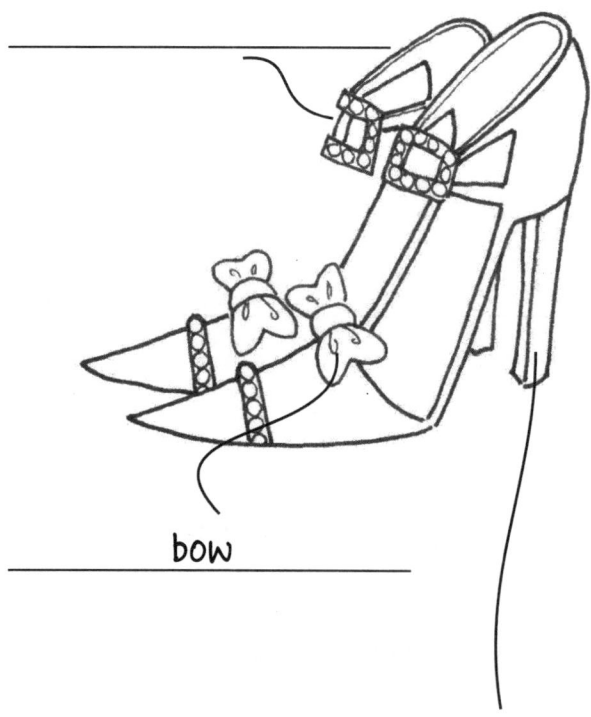

bow

6 Fantasy shoes

 A Draw one more feature onto the shoes above.

Choose from:
springs
wings
musical flowers
special powers

Unit review

A Write one sentence about each poem you have read in this unit. Use these sentence starters to help you:

I thought …   I remember …   I laughed when …

Poem: *Ask Mummy, Ask Daddy*

_____

Poem: *Younger Brother*

_____

Poem: *Tea with Aunty Mabel*

_____

Poem: *New Shoes*

_____

Poem: *Dinner-time Rhyme*

_____

B Make a honeycomb of words that rhyme with *shoe*. Add extra bits of honeycomb if you need to.

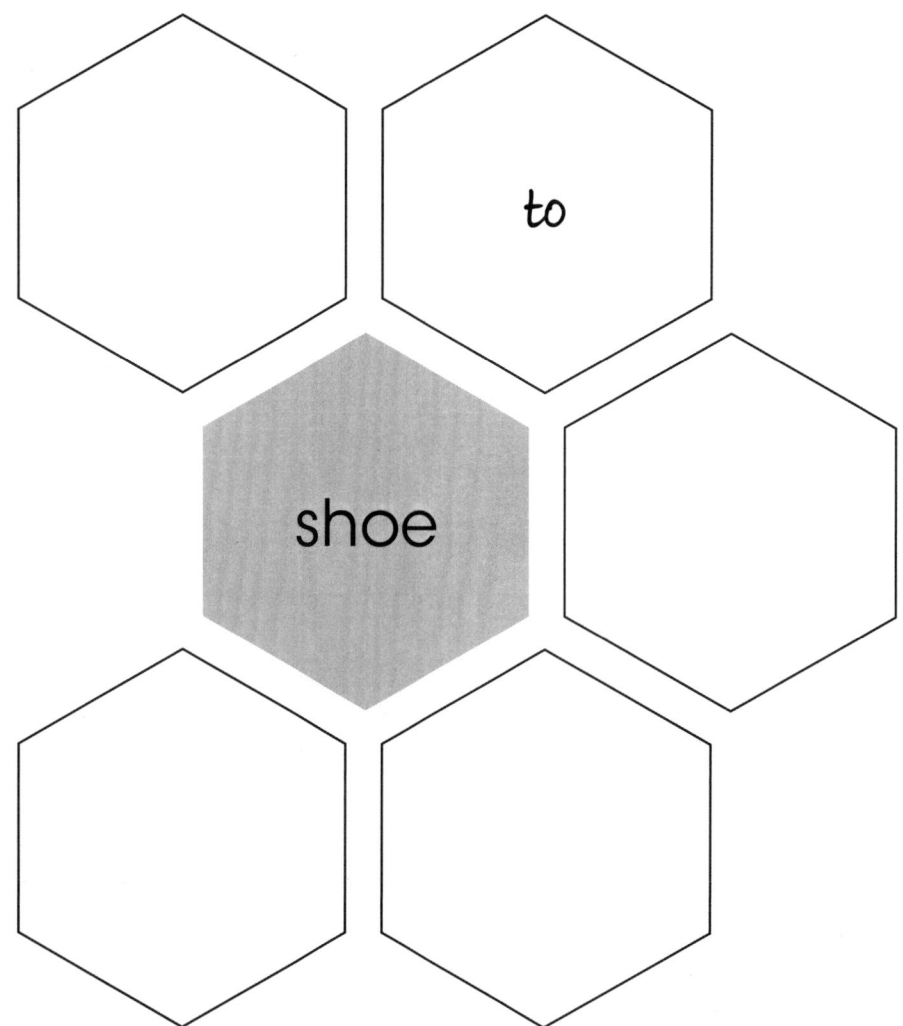

C Use capital letters in these poets' names.

Write how many syllables there are in each name.

john agard _____ ☐

trevor millum _____ ☐

june crebbin _____ ☐

jeanne willis _____ ☐

Unit 3 Rhymes about places and people we know

4 Tales from around the world

1 Choosing words

A Draw a tail in each box to match the description.

short and curly with a star on the end	soft, furry and very long
thick, straight and patterned	scaly, long and soft

B Write a description for each of these tails.

1 _____

_____

2 _____

_____

Session 1 Choosing words 37

2 Reading and understanding *How the Bear Lost His Tail*

A Read this part of the story. Find these words in the text and circle them.

| saw | was | dangling | looking | lying | trotting |
| sneaked | grabbed | tied | ran | met | caught | said |

1. Fox was trotting about one cold day, looking for something to eat.

2. He saw a fisherman by a frozen lake, dangling a line through a hole in the ice.

3. The fisherman had caught a lot of fish. They were lying in the snow, tied together with string. Fox was hungry.

4. Fox was sly and quick. He sneaked up, grabbed the string of fish, and ran as fast as he could!

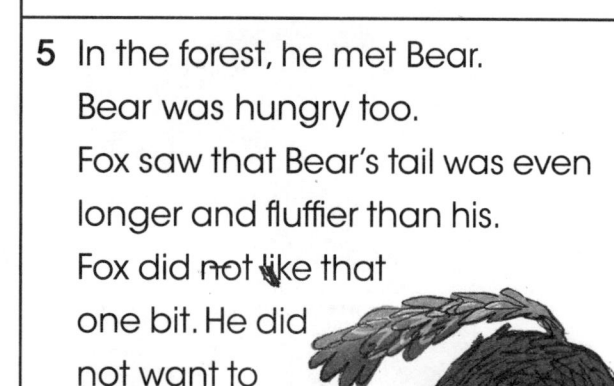

5. In the forest, he met Bear. Bear was hungry too. Fox saw that Bear's tail was even longer and fluffier than his. Fox did not like that one bit. He did not want to share his fish either.

6. So Fox said, "I caught these fish!" "How?" asked Bear. "All you have to do is break a hole in the ice on the lake," said Fox. "Then you sit down and put your tail in the water."

Adapted from *How the Bear Lost His Tail* by Susan Price and Sara Ogilvie

Unit 4 Tales from around the world

3 Retelling *How the Bear Lost His Tail*

A Write a sentence for each picture to tell this part of the story.

B Finish this sentence to end the story.

From that day to this …

Join your letters where you can.

Session 3 Retelling *How the Bear Lost his Tail*

4 Story themes

A Choose the right ending to finish the sentence. Make sure it compares one thing to another.

*Did you know when you say something is **like** something else, it is called a simile?*

As busy as a	fox
As high as a	cucumber
As strong as an	bee
As quick as a	tortoise
As slow as a	kite
As cool as a	ox

B Write similes of your own in the last two boxes.

Unit 4 Tales from around the world

5 Story summary

A Draw what you think the Shokpa looks like in his cave.

Label parts of his body. **Example:** *sharp teeth*

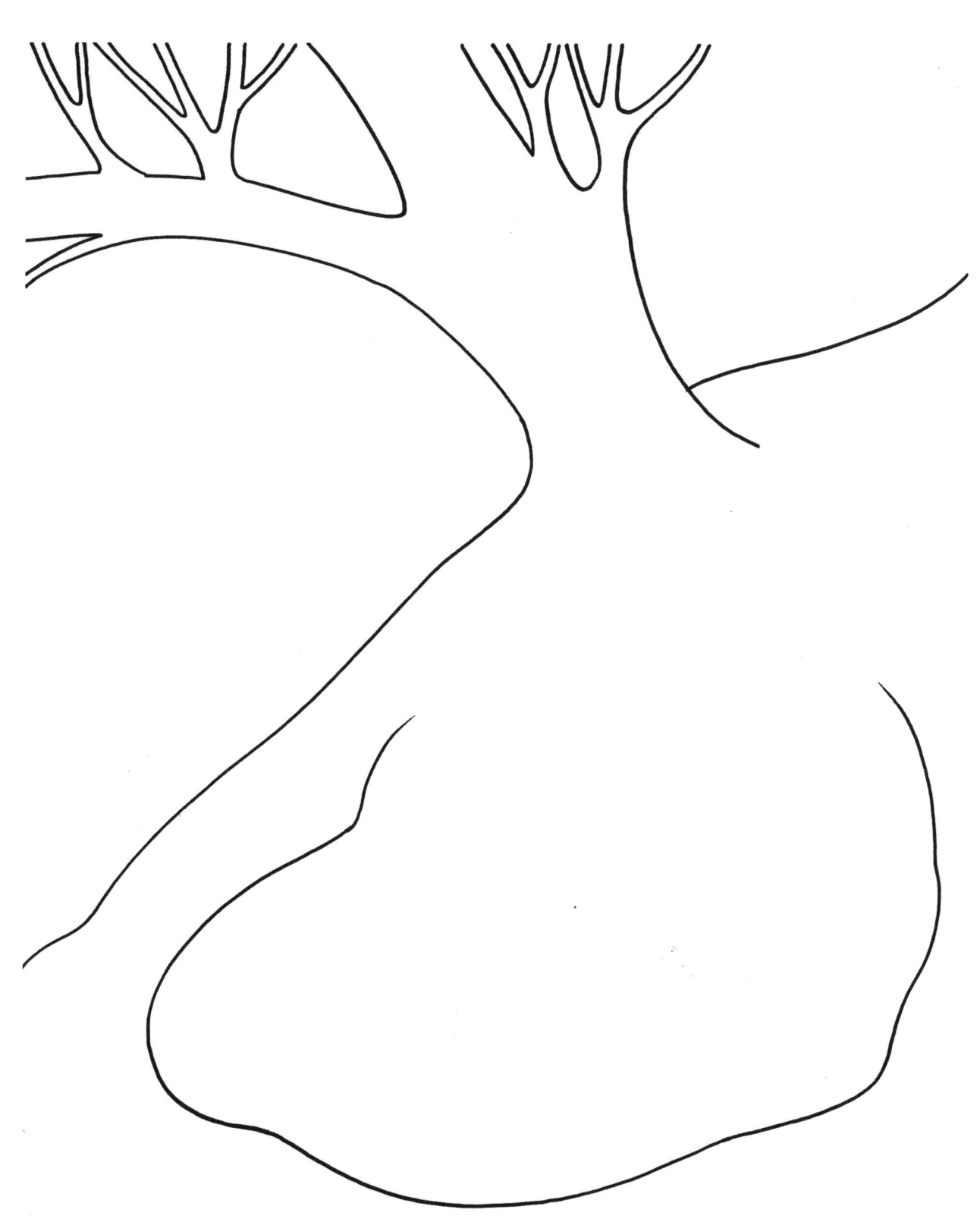

6 Checking understanding

A If you met a Shokpa what would you ask him?

Write three questions.

Have you remembered to begin your question with a capital letter and to end it with a question mark (?)

1 _____

2 _____

3 _____

B All these words have the prefixes **un** or **dis** at the beginning.

- How many of these words can you read in one minute? _____
- Ask someone to time you reading the words. Underline any that you had to 'pass' on.

unable	undo	untie	unroll	unkind
dislike	disagree	distrust	disorder	disappear
unafraid	unzip	unlit	uncut	unhappy

- Look them up in a dictionary (a book or online) if you do not know what they mean.

*Remember **un** or **dis** can mean <u>not</u>. – For example: I disagree means I do <u>not</u> agree.*

Unit 4 Tales from around the world

7 Exploring and writing

A Ask people in your family or friends what they would wish for.

Can you help to make their wish come true?

Name	Wish	Can you help them? Yes/No

B Read these sentences. Tick if they are true and put a cross if they are untrue.

Untrue and *false* mean the same thing. They are two words with the same meaning.

1 You can join sentences with the word *but*. ☐

2 You can join sentences with the word *the*. ☐

3 The Shokpa is a small animal that lives in trees. ☐

4 Another name for the Shokpa is the *Abominable Snowman*. ☐

5 Abominable means *pretty*. ☐

6 A woodcutter cuts wood. ☐

8 Yoshi the Stonecutter

A Write these names of countries with capital letters.

All words that are country names begin with a capital letter even if the word is in the middle of a sentence.

japan _____   brazil _____

england _____   china _____

india _____   poland _____

Write the name of your country here. _____

B Read these words from *Yoshi the Stonecutter*. Write the opposite meaning for each.

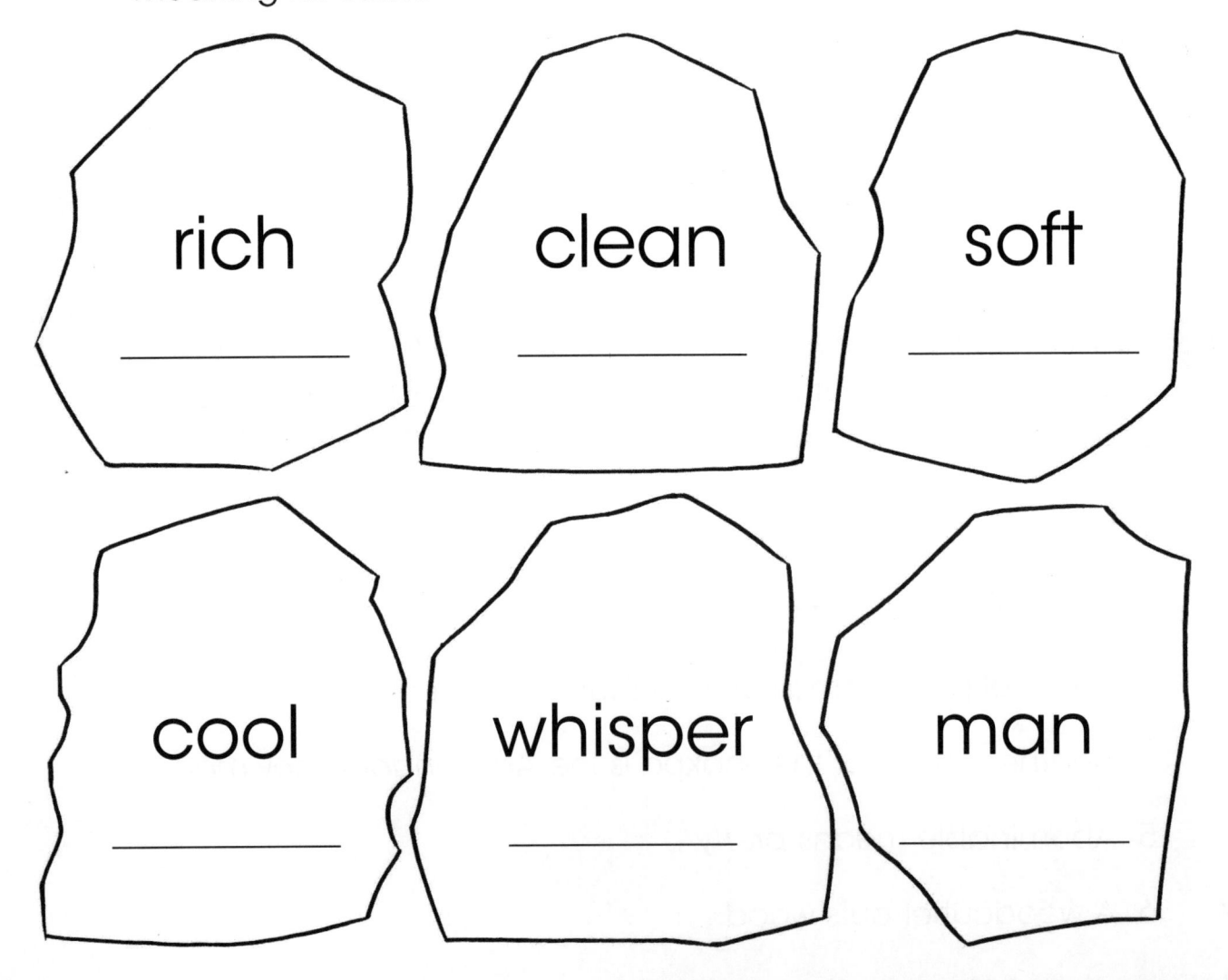

rich _____

clean _____

soft _____

cool _____

whisper _____

man _____

Unit 4 Tales from around the world

9 Speech in *Yoshi the Stonecutter*

A Add the speech marks to the sentences in the boxes.

The first one is done for you.

Yoshi speech	The whisper in the wind speech
"Oh I wish I could be a rich man," said Yoshi.	"Your wish is granted, Yoshi – a rich man you will be."
A prince is more powerful than a rich man. Oh I wish I could be a prince, said Yoshi.	Your wish is granted, Yoshi – a prince you will be.
The sun is more powerful than a prince. Oh I wish I could be the sun, said Yoshi.	Your wish is granted, Yoshi – the sun you will be.
A cloud is more powerful than the sun. Oh I wish I could be a cloud, said Yoshi.	Your wish is granted, Yoshi – a cloud you will be.

B Now read the story to a friend.

What can you do to make your reading aloud even better?

10 Finishing *Yoshi the Stonecutter*

A Fill in the gaps.

You can use words from the story or choose your own.

1 "Rocks are more _____ than clouds. I wish I could be a rock," _____ Yoshi.

2 "Your wish is _____, Yoshi – a rock you will be."

3 "A stonecutter is _____ than me! I wish I could be a man again," said Yoshi.

4 The _____ smiled, "Your wish is granted, Yoshi – a man you will be!"

46   Unit 4 Tales from around the world

B Change each sentence into the past tense by rewriting the underlined word. Try to use joined-up writing.

Language focus

We use the past tense to describe something that happened earlier or a long time ago. To make the past tense, we often add **ed**: *play – played*. But watch out! Sometimes the word changes completely: *go – went*.

1. Yoshi <u>is</u> a stonecutter.

   <u>Yoshi was a stonecutter.</u>

2. The "whisper in the wind" <u>smiles</u> at Yoshi.

   _____

3. Yoshi the rock <u>feels</u> the tools cutting into him.

   _____

4. The "whisper in the wind" <u>grants</u> Yoshi all his wishes.

   _____

5. Yoshi the stonecutter <u>picks</u> up his tools and <u>starts</u> to work.

   _____

11 Story shape

A Draw a picture in each circle to show what Yoshi wishes for.

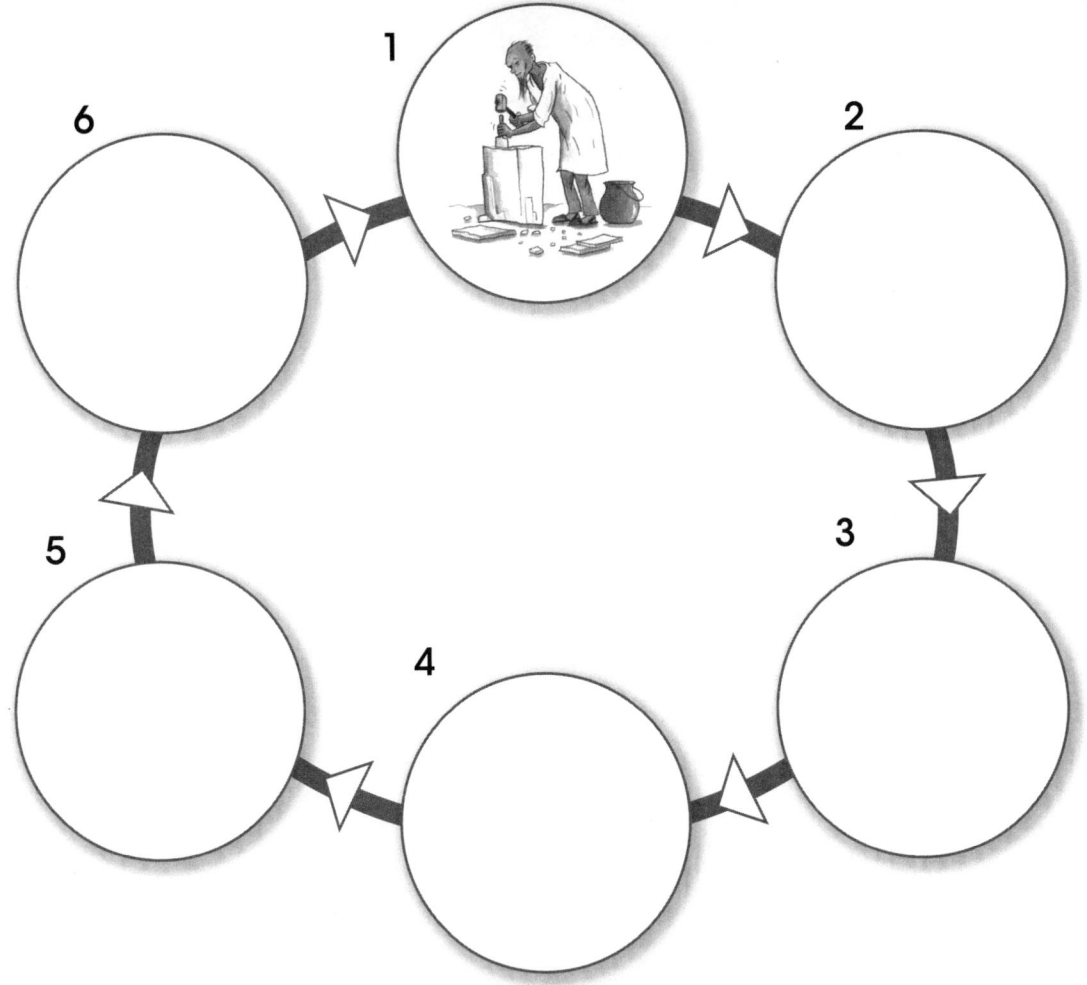

B Read all of the words. In each line, there is **one** word that is the odd one out.

Cross the word out.

1 grey   granted   Yoshi   great

2 yelled   whispered   grumbled   rain

3 cried   replied   said   tried

4 whisper   rock   white   wish

5 greedy   unhappy   bored   stonecutter

48 Unit 4 Tales from around the world

12 Reviewing the stories

A Write *true* or *false*.

1 Traditional tales can have animals that can talk. _____

2 There are no people in traditional tales. _____

3 Traditional tales sometimes have clever and silly characters.

_____

B Write your own quiz questions about traditional tales on these quiz cards.

Test a friend or someone in your family.

Unit review

A Make a honeycomb of your favourite words from this unit. Add extra bits of honeycomb if you need to.

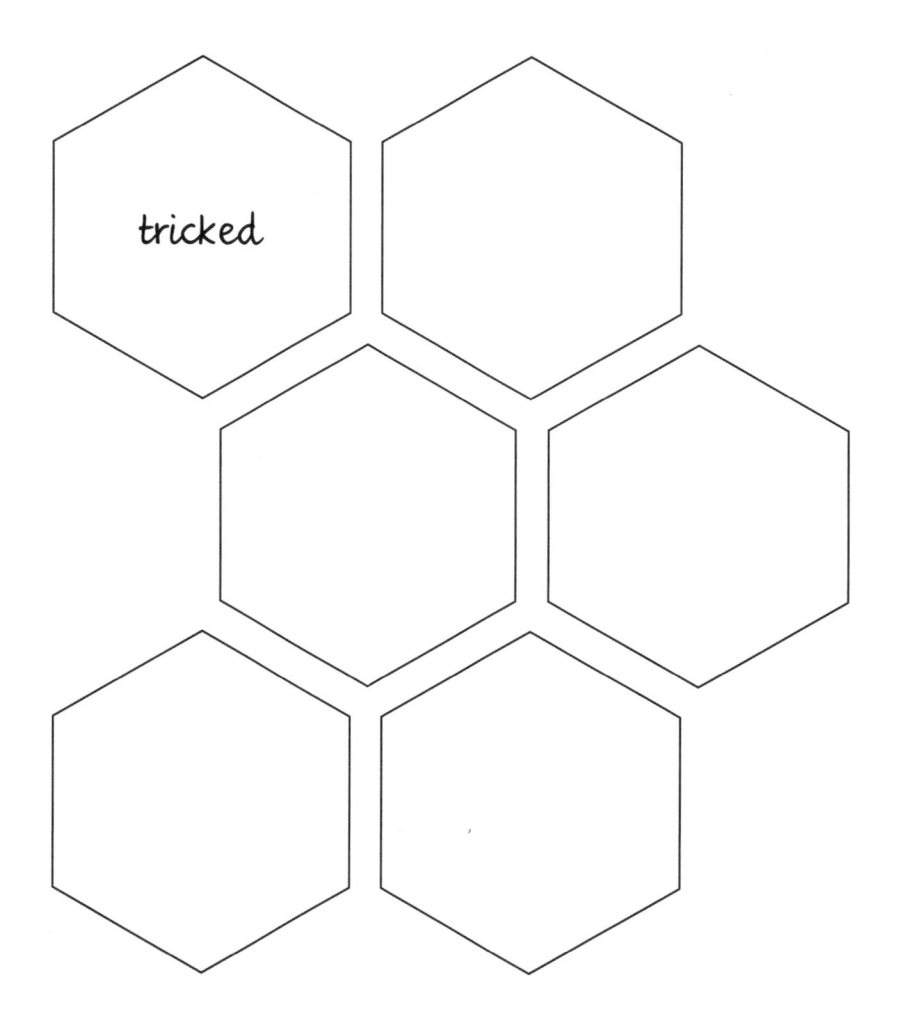

tricked

B Make a honeycomb of words about language that you need to remember from this unit. Here are some to remind you:

> adjective   simile   joining words   prefix   opposites   prediction
> story shape   circular story   speech marks   past tense

Only write the word in the honeycomb if you can say what it means. If you don't know, look back in the unit to find examples.

Add extra bits to the honeycomb if you need to.

Unit 4 Tales from around the world

adjective

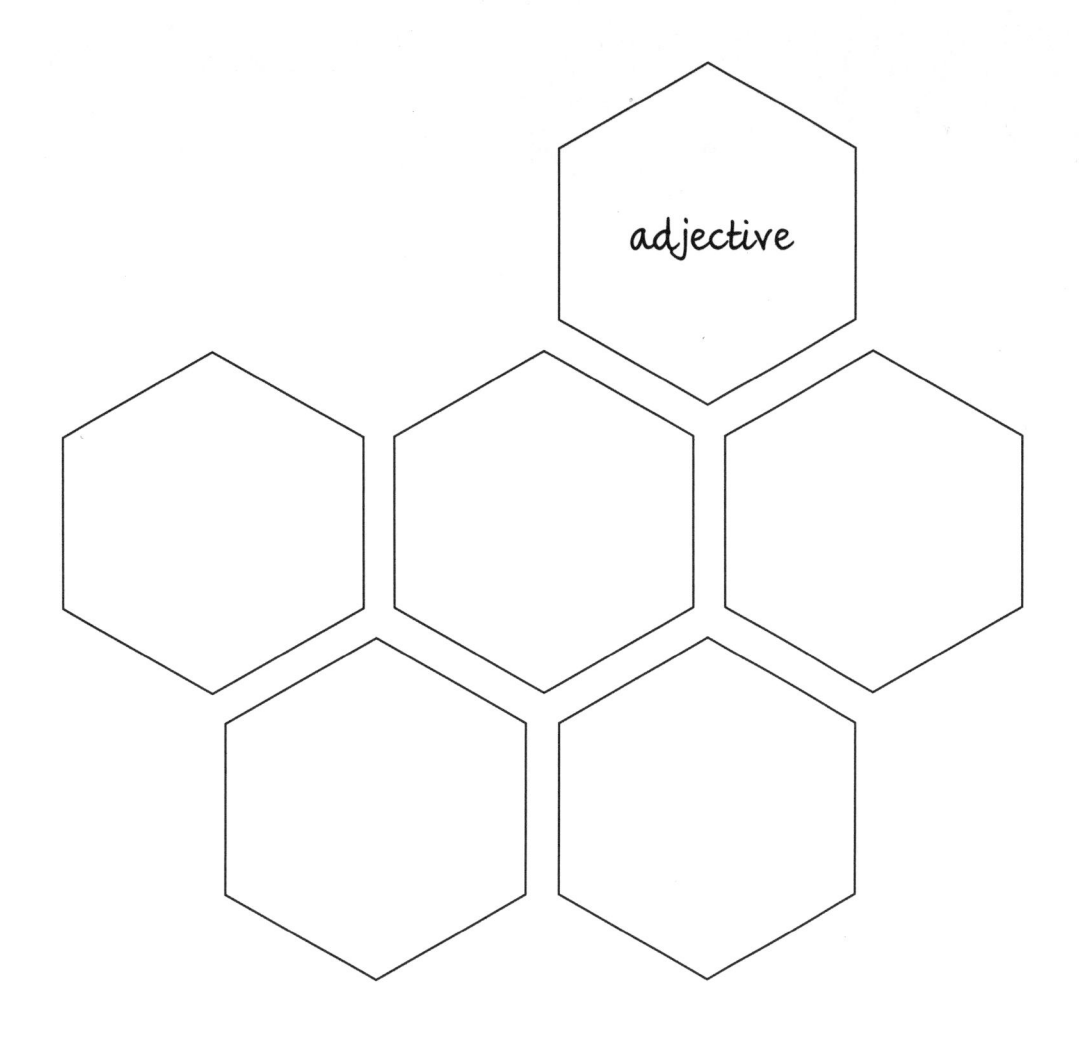

C Draw your favourite character from the unit. Write a sentence about him or her.

Unit review

5 What is my house made of?

1 What is your house made from?

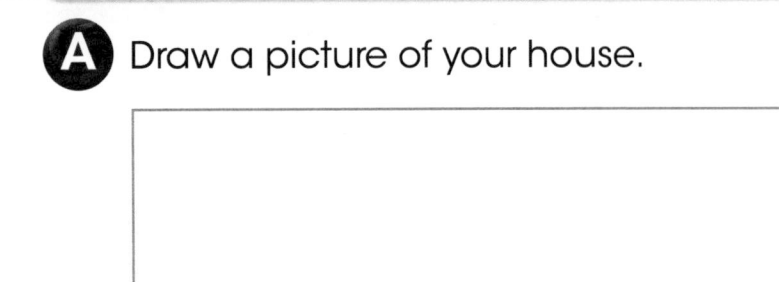

A Draw a picture of your house.

Write labels to show the building materials used to build your house. Use some of the words in the box:

bricks
concrete
glass
wood
steel
stone

B Finish spelling the **wh** question words. They are:

what, where, when, who, why, which and *how.*

Each word is written more than once.

__ __ a t   __ __ o   w h __ n

w h __ r __   h __ __   __ __ y

__ __ __ __ h   __ __ o   w h e __

__ __ a __   __ __ w   w h i __ __

__ __ e r __   w h __

Unit 5 What is my house made of?

2 Roofs

A How many times can you find the word *roofs* in one minute?
Circle them all as quickly as you can.

Why do houses need roofs?

Roofs help to keep people safe by protecting them from the weather. Roofs are on top of the house so they can give shelter from rain, cold winds and the hot sun.

How are roofs different?

In some countries where there is a lot of rain, roofs are built with slopes on them so the rain goes down the slope and onto the ground.

In hot, sunny countries people need roofs to provide shade during the day. Sometimes, the roofs are flat so that people can enjoy sitting on them in the evenings when it is not too hot. Some people sleep on the roofs of their houses.

B In each line, there is **one** word that does **not** have the same vowel sound as the underlined word. Cross the word out that doesn't match the sound.

sleep	need	slept	speech
speak	feather	each	bean
people	these	evening	enter
field	tie	chief	ceiling

3 Finding information from diagrams and charts

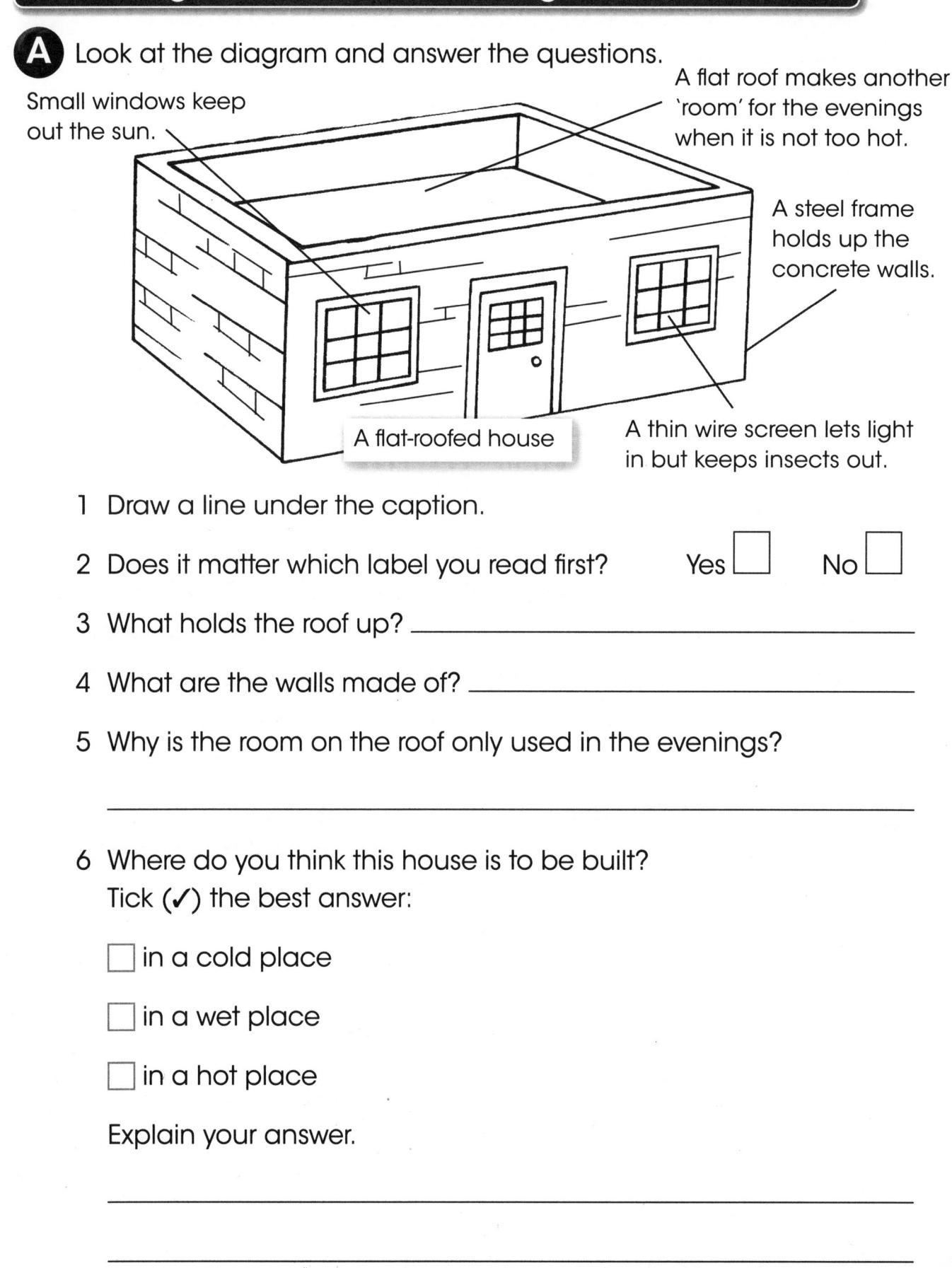

A Look at the diagram and answer the questions.

Small windows keep out the sun.

A flat roof makes another 'room' for the evenings when it is not too hot.

A steel frame holds up the concrete walls.

A thin wire screen lets light in but keeps insects out.

A flat-roofed house

1 Draw a line under the caption.

2 Does it matter which label you read first? Yes ☐ No ☐

3 What holds the roof up? _____

4 What are the walls made of? _____

5 Why is the room on the roof only used in the evenings?

_____

6 Where do you think this house is to be built?
   Tick (✓) the best answer:

   ☐ in a cold place

   ☐ in a wet place

   ☐ in a hot place

   Explain your answer.

   _____

   _____

Unit 5 What is my house made of?

B Write *and, but, so* or *or* to join the sentences.

1 Houses have windows _____ houses have doors.

2 A house can have a flat roof _____ it can have a sloped roof.

3 A house has a sloped roof _____ the rain can fall off it.

4 Light can come in through windows _____ insects can come in too.

5 The house has a flat roof _____ people can walk on it safely.

6 Iron is strong enough to hold up a roof _____ paper is not strong enough.

4 Reading explanations

A Add eight full stops to this text. Write a capital letter at the start of each new sentence.

people have been building huts from grass, mud and clay for a very long time because these materials have always been easy to find builders look for wood as well because trees are strong enough to hold up the roof

the wooden frame of a house needs to be built first then people start using mud and clay to make the walls in hot countries the mud walls dry very quickly but it takes longer in cold countries sometimes, people make the mud stronger by weaving in animal hairs

finally, the builder makes a wooden frame for the roof and starts laying grass on top of the frame the grasses must all be laid in the same direction so that rain will trickle off

B Answer these questions about the text.

1 Write a title for the text. _____

2 Tick (✓) the features you can find in the text:

☐ It explains *how* or *why* something happens.

☐ One piece of the explanation leads into the next so you must read the text in the order it is written.

☐ It is written in the present tense.

☐ It has headings, labels, captions or diagrams.

3 Do you think it was a good explanation text? Tick (✓) the answer.

☐ Yes

☐ No

Explain why. _____

_____

_____

4 Do you think this piece of writing would make someone want to read the text? Tick (✓) the answer.

☐ Yes

☐ No

Explain why. _____

_____

_____

5 Using a dictionary

a b c d e f g h i j k l m n o p q r s t u v w x y z

A Add these animal names to the alphabetical list of animals.

iguana   giraffe   lion   zebra   snake   dog

ant	monkey
bear	octopus
cat	panda
elephant	rat
frog	tiger
hippopotamus	walrus
kangaroo	yak

Write the alphabet. _____

_____

Session 5 Using a dictionary

6 Writing longer definitions

A Read all of the information given. Cross out the piece of information that is not useful. Draw or write what is being described.

Read the information. Cross out something that is not useful.	Draw what is being described.

1 It is red.
    It has four wheels.
    It goes fast.
    I saw it on Rochor Canal Road.	

2 The lights are shiny.
    It has three lights.
    It can control the traffic.
    It can help you drive safely.	

3 It has four wheels.
    It is used to push babies around.
    It has a handle.
    It had a baby boy in it.	

4 It has two wheels.
    It belongs to Mr Farrer.
    It has a saddle.
    It has a handlebar.	

5 People buy things there.
    It sells fruit.
    It sells vegetables too.
    I like mangoes best.	

Unit 5 What is my house made of?

B Write a longer sentence about each of the things, using the information from the table.

> Remember, you can use: *and, so,* or *but* to join shorter sentences.

For example: It is red and it has four wheels.

1 _____

2 _____

3 _____

4 _____

5 _____

7 Finding the main idea

A Read the text. Tick (✓) the main idea in each paragraph.

Houses on the move

1 Some people don't stay in one place all of the time, so they don't stay in houses. This might be for a holiday, or it might be for work, or it might be for another reason.

Tick the main idea:
a People go on holiday and leave their homes behind. ☐
b People like taking their own things with them when they move around. ☐
c Some people don't always stay in houses because they have to move around. ☐

2 For 3000 years yurts have been used by people in central Asia when they move around to look for food for their animals. Yurts have a round wooden frame with a thick felt cover to keep the space inside warm. A family can pack their yurt onto camels very quickly so they can move to another place.

Tick the main idea:
a   Yurts are very old. ☐
b   People in central Asia use yurts when they travel around. ☐
c   Yurts have a wooden frame with a felt cover. ☐

3 In warmer places, like in the desert, people live in tents while they travel with their animals. The tents are more for shelter than for warmth, so the covering may be thinner. Tents are made of cloth over a wooden frame.

Tick the main idea:
a   People who travel in the desert live in tents. ☐
b   Tents are lighter than yurts. ☐
c   People have animals in the desert. ☐

4 In frozen places, seal hunters build an igloo as an overnight shelter when they are away from home. The hunter carves blocks of ice and builds a dome out of ice.

Tick the main idea:
a   Seal hunters have to carry knives. ☐
b   Igloos are dome-shaped. ☐
c   Igloos are overnight shelters for hunters. ☐

B Finish these words which have the **or** sound.
Use letters from the box.

c _a_ _l_ l   f __ __ k   w __ __ k   d r __ __

m __ __ __   f __ __ l   s p __ __ t

s __ __ c e   c r __ __ l   number f __ __ __

| or |
| ore |
| al |
| au |
| aw |
| our |

8 Making notes

A Look back at the *Houses on the Move* text. Write notes next to the pictures.

Yurts

_____
_____
_____

Tents

_____
_____
_____

Igloos

_____
_____
_____

How to make notes
- Write only the most important words. Choose the words which give the main idea.
- Leave out words like *the, a* and *of*.
- You don't have to write in sentences.

9 Planning an oral explanation

A Use *and*, *but*, *so* or *or* to fill the gaps.

1 Children can't build big buildings _____ they can build dens.

2 Building dens can be complicated _____ you have to plan them carefully.

3 You can buy little tents _____ you can build your own den.

4 You can play in your den _____ you can let your friend play with you.

B Look at these words: *put, very, people, called, asked, want.*

Write each of the words inside its shape.

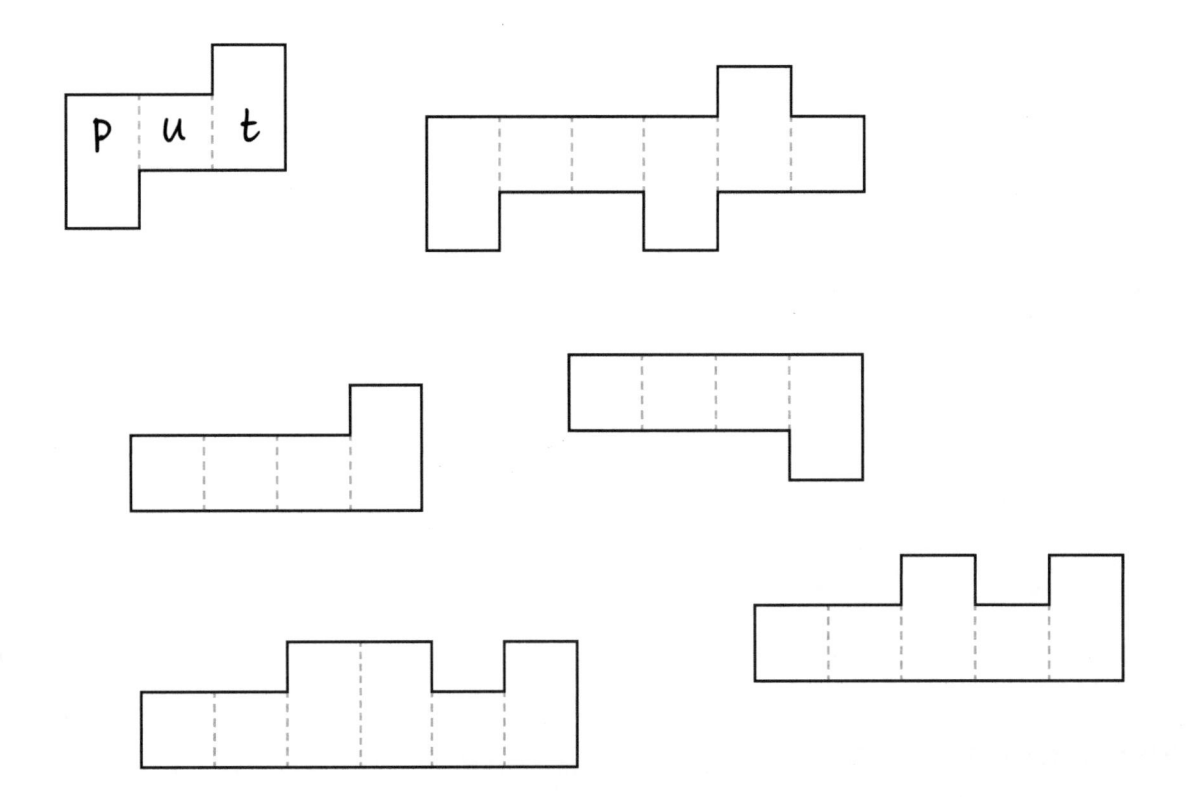

p u t

Unit 5 What is my house made of?

10 Presenting an oral explanation

A Think about the talk you gave and the talks you listened to. Draw 😊 or ☹ to show how well you did.

My talk	😊 or ☹
My speaking	
I spoke loudly and clearly.	
I used expression.	
I tried to make it interesting for my listeners.	
My listening	
I looked at the speaker.	
I sat still.	
I thought about what I heard and asked questions.	

I am happy with:

_____

_____

I need to get better at:

_____

_____

B Draw lines between pairs of words that have the same long vowel sound.

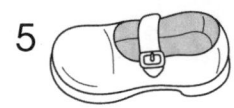

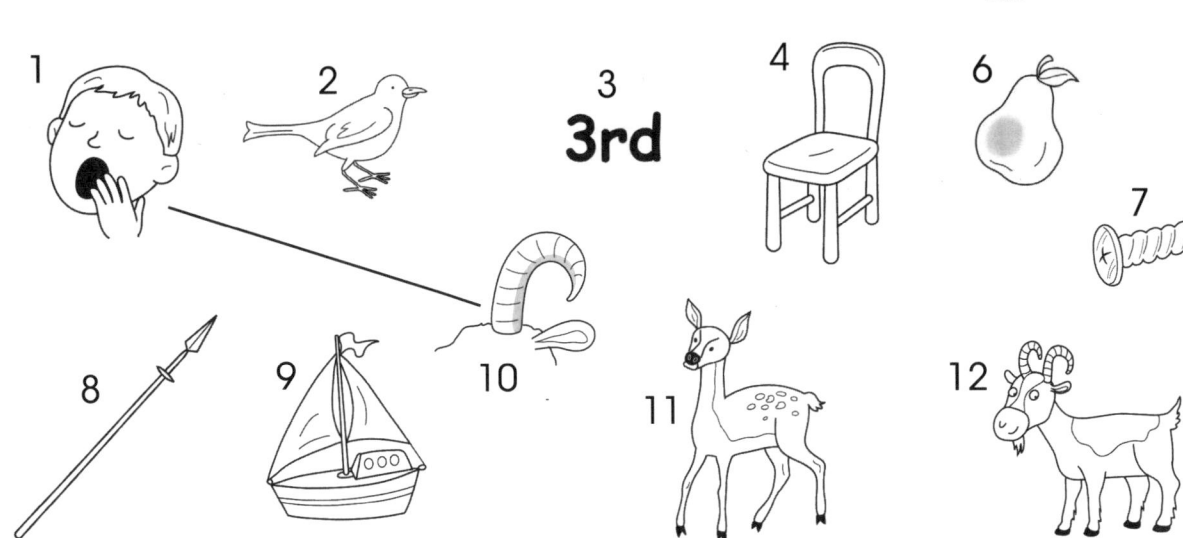

11 Writing an explanation

A How many times can you find the word **boat** or **houseboat** in this text in one minute?

Circle the words.

Houseboats

All around the world, people live in structures that are not buildings. Some people live in houseboats. A houseboat is a boat that has been changed a bit to allow people to live in it.

In Kerala, in Southern India, houseboats are about 18–21 m (60–70 feet) long. They are slow-moving barges that were used to carry rice and spices. It took a long time for the boat to make a voyage so the family had to live in the boat too.

Floating village

A place called Aberdeen is one of the most important fishing ports in Hong Kong. The island of Hong Kong is very crowded so for over 100 years, fishermen have been living on their fishing boats – or junks – in the port. Over 6000 people live in 600 junks in Aberdeen floating village.

Canal life

Canals are rivers made by people. Canals are like roads in the city of Amsterdam in Holland so some people live on houseboats on the canals. Some houseboats are even hotels! The houseboats usually have gardens on them. They are big enough to have up to three bedrooms.

B Answer the questions.

1 Why did people in Kerala start living on boats?

_____

_____

2 Why is it so hard to find somewhere to live in Hong Kong?

_____

3 Who lives in the floating village?

_____

4 What is another word for Hong Kong fishing boats? _____

5 What is a canal?

_____

6 What are houseboats in Amsterdam like?

_____

_____

7 Cross out the word that is **not** a boat.

barge   port   junk   houseboat

Session 11 Writing an explanation

12 Improving writing

A Tick (✓) the statements that are true about the *Houseboats* text on pages 64–65.

☐ It is a story.

☐ It is an explanation.

☐ It is written mainly in the present tense.

☐ It is written mainly in the past tense.

☐ It explains why something happens.

☐ It tells you how to do something.

☐ The text needs to be read in order because the information builds up and tells you what happens next.

☐ The text can be read in any order.

☐ The headings introduce the subject of the next part of the text.

☐ There is a heading at the beginning of each paragraph.

☐ The pictures help to explain what the text is about.

☐ The pictures make the text easier to read.

B Write three things you didn't know before you read the *Houseboats* text.

_____

_____

_____

Unit 5 What is my house made of?

Unit review

A Write these words into the crossword.

Write one letter in each box.

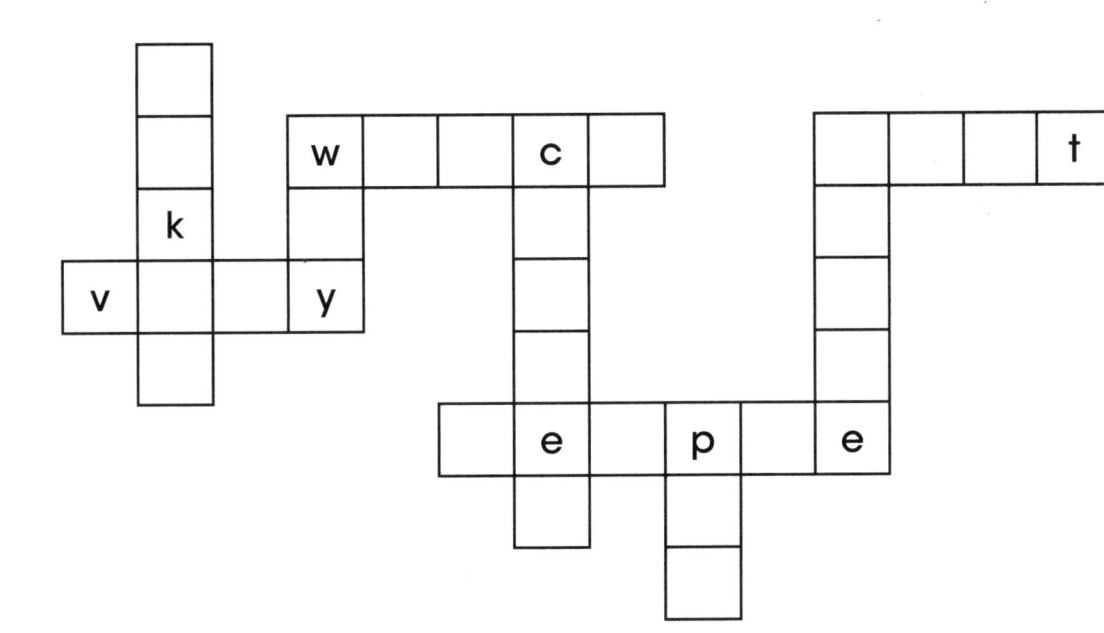

want
where
why
which
put
very
people
called
asked

B Look at the pictures and write the words.

Tip

Here are some common spellings for each sound:

or: or, ore, aw, al, au

ar: ar

ur: ur, ir, or, ear

6 Poems by famous poets

1 Word play

A Write the missing words and then read the poem again.

It is not the whole poem, just part of it.

Busy Day by Michael Rosen

Pop in
pop _____
pop _____ the road
pop _____ for a walk
pop _____ to the shop
can't stop
got to pop
got to pop?
pop where?
pop what?

well
I've got to
pop _____
pop _____
pop _____ to town
pop _____ and see
pop _____ for tea
pop _____ to the shop
can't stop
got to pop

Use each of these words once:
out over down up out
out in down round in

All of the missing words are about direction and movement.

Unit 6 Poems by famous poets

B Copy out these three lines from the poem. Use your best handwriting. Join the letters if you can.

got to pop? _____

pop where? _____

pop what? _____

Tip
The poet has not used capital letters at all in this poem but he has used question marks. Copy them carefully.

2 Strange Journey

A Remember the poem *Riding down to Boxland* by Michael Rosen. It tells a story.

Sort these lines from the poem into the right order to tell the story. Use numbers 1–5.

1	Riding down to boxland where people live in boxes,
☐	laid it out at home, no-one looked inside
☐	no answer from inside, I picked up the box
☐	saw a box looking good, I knocked on the lid,
☐	Riding back from boxland the box coming with me,

B Write two new lines for this poem.

_____

_____

3 Exploring Rhythm

A On Julia Donaldson's *The Food Train*, there was:

- coffee
- bread and butter
- biscuits and cheese
- fish and chips
- soup.

What would you choose for your food train?

_____

_____

B Find two words from the boxes that have the same vowel sound in them even though they don't rhyme.

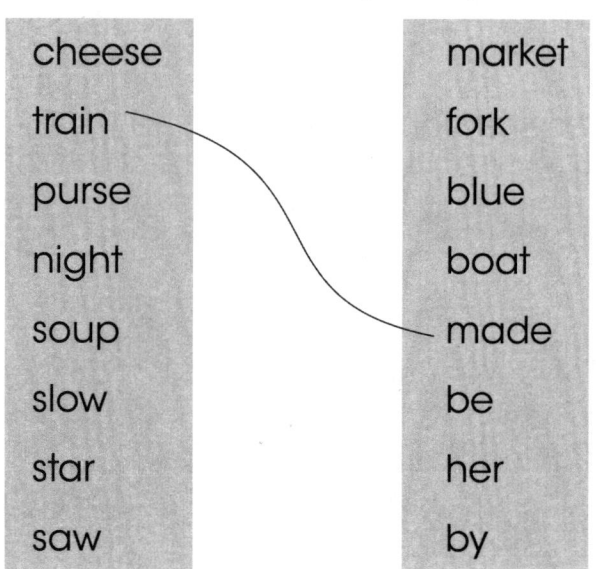

cheese	market
train	fork
purse	blue
night	boat
soup	made
slow	be
star	her
saw	by

I know! *Train* and *made* both have the **ai** sound in them.

C Ask someone to time you reading the words below. Underline any that you had to 'pass' on.

don't	old	by	house	about	asked
here	called	said	there	want	where
who	why	which	put	very	people

How many of these words did you read in one minute? _____

Unit 6 Poems by famous poets

4 Shape poems

A Read Roger McGough's poem, *Downhill Racer*, again.

Write the missing rhyming words:
- *slide*, *side* and *glide*
- *ease*, *skis*.

With a coloured pencil, draw a line between the words to show the shape better.

Downhill Racer

Down
    the
        snow
           white
      page
we
_____.
  From
      side
        to
          _____
      we
_____.
      Pass
        obstacles
           with
              _____.
          Words
        on
_____.
Look out.
    Here
      comes
    a
    poem
      in
    a
      hurry!

Session 4 Shape poems

5 The River's a ...

A Read this part of Valerie Bloom's poem, *The River*, again.

The River's a hoarder,
And he buries down deep
Those little treasures
That he wants to keep.

Answer these questions:

1 What *little treasures* do you think the River likes to keep?
   _____

2 How does the River bury them *down deep*?
   _____

3 How does this make the River sound as a character?
   _____

6 Writing like Valerie Bloom

A Draw what sort of person or animal you think the River is like.

Add some notes to explain what sort of person you think it is.
_____

Unit review

A What are some of the words and features you have learned to help you to talk about poems?

Label this poem with the right words from the box.

> rhyming words   poet   title   like an animal
> like an animal   words repeated

The Sea

The sea is a hungry dog,
giant and grey
he rolls on the beach all day.
with his clashing teeth and shaggy jaws
hour after hour he gnaws
the rumbling, rumbling stones,
and 'bones, bones, bones!'
the giant sea-dog moans,
licking his greasy paws.

James Reeves

B Describe the layout of the poem.

_____

_____

7 Stories by famous writers

1 What do you like to read?

A Draw a picture about a book that you have enjoyed reading.

Write the title.

_____

_____

Write about what you read.

_____

_____

B Look at these pictures. Finish the word using one of these endings: **er, ar, or, our** or **ure**. Then write the whole word using joined-up handwriting underneath.

flow ___ ___   danc ___ ___   doct ___ ___   pict ___ ___ ___

_____   _____   _____   _____

writ ___ ___   hamm ___ ___   tig ___ ___   caterpill ___ ___

_____   _____   _____   _____

auth ___ ___   harb ___ ___ ___   vult ___ ___ ___   fing ___ ___

_____   _____   _____   _____

Session 1 What do you like to read?   75

2 Introducing *The Hodgeheg* by Dick King-Smith

A Read more about Max the Hodgeheg.

Max has gone out of his garden to try to find out how humans cross the road safely.

[1] At last he began to feel rather tired and to think how nice it would be to go home to bed. But which way was home?
Max considered this and came to the unhappy conclusion [2] that he was lost. Just then he saw, not far away, a hedgehog crossing the path, a large hedgehog, a Pa-sized hedgehog! [3] What luck! Pa had crossed the street to find him! He ran forward, but when he reached the animal he found he was a complete stranger.
[4] "Oh," said Max. "I peg your bardon. I thought you were a different hodgeheg."
The stranger looked curiously at him.
"Are you feeling all right?" he said.
"Yes, thanks," said Max. "Trouble is, I go to want home. But I won't know the day."

B Answer the questions.

1 Tick (✓) the statement that describes what is happening in this part of the story.

☐ Max is at home in bed.

☐ Max is looking for Pa.

☐ Max is looking for other hedgehogs.

☐ Max is lost.

2 Which words tell the reader that Max has been walking for a long time?

　

3 Why did Max run towards the other hedgehog?

　

4 Why did the stranger ask Max if he was feeling all right?

　

Give an example.

　

5 What do you think Max wanted the stranger to do?

　

6 List the **wh** question words used in questions 2 to 5.

　　　　　　　　

C Look for the little numbers in the text, e.g.¹. Draw lines to show how Max was feeling at each number.

Number	Feeling
1	unhappy
2	tired
3	disappointed
4	relieved

3 Language in *The Hodgeheg*

A Fill in the gaps using *and, but, or, so* or *because*.

Max the hedgehog wanted to learn how to cross a road safely _____ so many hedgehogs were killed on the road. He wanted to know what to do _____ he could tell other hedgehogs _____ they would all live longer.

Max tried to find the places where people crossed the road _____ those places weren't always good crossing places for hedgehogs. He kept on getting hurt _____ getting lost _____ getting in the way.

At last, Max found the best place for hedgehogs to cross the road safely. He took his sisters _____ they could try it too.

B Read the words. If you can add **ly**, write the new word. If you can't add **ly**, cross out the word.

kind	~~eat~~	bad	blue	brave
kindly	_____	_____	_____	_____

cross	deep	even	glad	hate
_____	_____	_____	_____	_____

love	near	quiet	run	slow
_____	_____	_____	_____	_____

Unit 7 Stories by famous writers

4 Introducing *The Lost Happy Endings* by Carol Ann Duffy

A Re-read the story.

Jub's job was important and she was very proud of it. Each evening when dusk was removing the outline of things, like a rubber, Jub had to shoulder her big green sack and carry all the Happy Endings of stories from one end of the forest to the other in time for everybody's bedtime. Once she had reached the edge of the forest, Jub had to climb to the top of a huge old oak tree, still with her sack on her back, and sit on the tallest branch. Then, very carefully, Jub would open the sack and shake out the happy endings into the violet evening air. She was good at this because she had six fingers on each small hand.

B Use information in the story to draw a picture of Jub shaking out the happy endings. Write labels to show the information you used.

C Write tricky words in the grid. Write one letter in each box. Use these words:

> could because most every pretty
> sure after many their would

5 Language in *The Lost Happy Endings*

A Look at the picture of Jub.

Write five interesting words to describe her and five interesting words to describe where she is.

Words to describe Jub:

_____

_____

_____

_____

_____

Words about where Jub is:

_____

_____

_____

_____

_____

Don't forget to use question marks (?) at the end of your questions.

B Make up six questions about the picture.

1 Who _____

2 Where _____

3 What _____

4 When _____

5 Why _____

6 How _____

Session 5 Language in *The Lost Happy Endings*

6 Likes and dislikes

A Would you like to read more about Jub? **Yes / No**

Explain your answer. Give at least three reasons.

_____

_____

_____

_____

_____

B Underline every time you use *and, but, because, so, or* or *in* your answer.

7 Introducing *Little Albatross* by Michael Morpurgo

A Read these words from *Little Albatross*. Think about the sound made by the underlined vowel. Write the word in the correct box.

<u>a</u>lbatross   <u>a</u>lways   f<u>a</u>ther   fl<u>a</u>shing   w<u>a</u>ndering   w<u>a</u>tching

a sounds like apple	**a** sounds like orange
a sounds like cart	**a** sounds like fork

Unit 7 Stories by famous writers

c**o**me m**o**ther **o**ne **o**ver str**o**ng
s**o** s**o**ng t**o** t**o**p **o**wn wh**o**

o sounds like **o**range	o sounds like **u**p
o sounds like b**oa**t	o sounds like b**oo**t

B Complete the words below with **ear**, **eer** or **ere**.

They all have a vowel sound like in *hear*.

1 "Come h_____ and get your book," said the teacher.

2 The class gave a ch_____ when Raphael won the race.

3 The man had a big, bushy b_____d.

4 Some people use sp_____s when they hunt.

5 A d_____ is an animal which lives in a herd.

Complete the words below with **air**, **ear** or **are**.

They all have a vowel sound like in *hair*.

6 She sat on her ch_____ under a p_____ tree.

7 B_____s live in caves in the mountains.

8 The little girl had b_____ feet.

9 When you get on a bus, you have to pay the f_____ .

10 "It's not f_____ !" shouted the little boy.

8 Language in *Little Albatross*

A The author uses groups of words with the same sounds in them.

*Out over the **s**urging **s**ea they **s**oared, always on the look-out for **s**ilver fla**sh**ing fi**sh s**wimming below them in the **s**urging **s**ea.*

Try writing another word with the same sound to describe these animals.

For example: __enormous__ elephant

__t_____ tiger   _____ lion

_____ snake   _____ penguin

_____ crocodile   _____ horse

B Draw lines to join the everyday words to the more interesting words that share the same meaning.

Everyday words	Interesting words
walked	hovered
said	strolled
took	announced
flew	gobbled
ate	snoozed
slept	snatched

9 Paragraphs

A Look at the story mountain

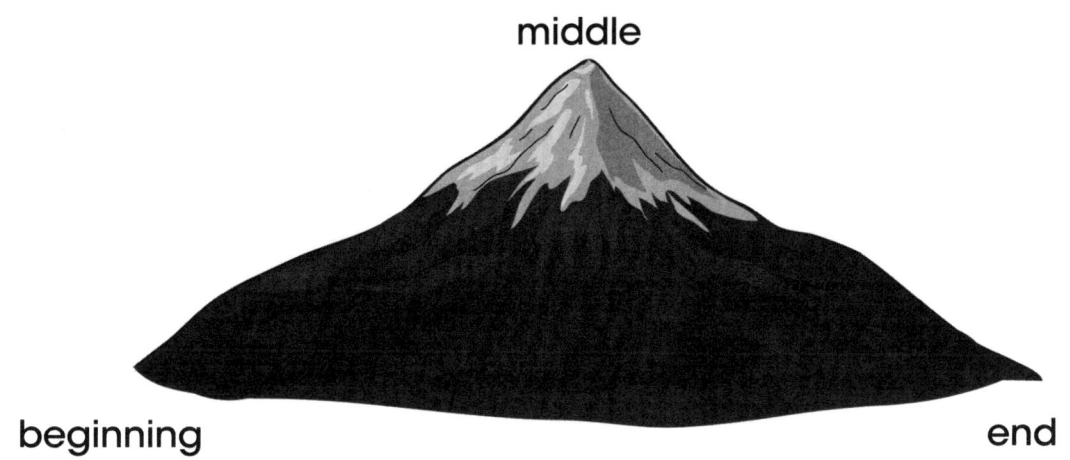

middle

beginning　　　　　　　　　　　　　　　　　end

Write the name of a story you know well. _____

Write about one or two events that happen in each part of this story.

Part of story	Event or events
Beginning	
Middle	
End	

Language focus

A suffix is a group of letters added to the end of a word. Most suffixes change the meaning of the words.

- Baby Albatross felt hope**ful** because he thought his parents would come home.
- Baby Albatross felt hope**less** because he was all alone and didn't know if his parents would return.

*Even though the suffix **ful** means 'full of', it is only spelled with one **l**.*

B Add the suffix **ful** or **less** in the gaps.

1. She used lots of colours to create a colour―――― picture.
2. Gina was very care―――― as she coloured her picture in neatly.
3. Mummy felt help―――― when she couldn't comfort her crying child.
4. The kittens were very play―――― after their sleep.
5. Most spiders are harm―――― although some are dangerous.

10 Planning your own story

A Look at the storyboard.

Unit 7 Stories by famous writers

In each of the boxes, write a word or group of words to tell the reader *when* the events happen. You could use words from the box below or choose your own.

1	2	3

> Later   Early one morning   One hot day
> At last   Suddenly   When the sun was setting
> After that   Eventually   Without warning

B Write **three** words to describe each character. Use words from the box or choose your own.

> worried   interested   relieved   whimpering
> galloping   attacking   prowling   frightened
> calmed   upset   curious   distressed   hungry
> roaring   pouncing   anxious   comforted   racing

- the baby zebra _____ _____ _____

- the adult zebra _____ _____ _____

- the lion _____ _____ _____

Write a sentence about the setting.

_____

Session 10 Planning your own story

11 Writing your story

A Look again at the storyboard. Choose one character in each of the pictures. Draw a speech bubble from their mouth and write what they might be saying.

B Read this paragraph from the zebra story. Cross out any sentences that don't belong in the paragraph.

> Mother and Father Zebra were far away looking for food. They were sure no lions would come near their baby. Lions live in Africa. You can sometimes see them in zoos. Then suddenly Mother Zebra heard a distant roar, followed by a whimper from her baby. She was very worried. Baby lions don't have manes. She knew they had to get back as quickly as possible.

12 Improving your story

A Write the opening paragraph of the zebra story. Remember what you have learned from writing your story in class.

Unit 7 Stories by famous writers

B Write the ending of the zebra story. It needs to be exciting. Remember to use the dialogue you planned in Session 11.

_____

_____

_____

_____

_____

Unit review

A Look at these words:

> after   because   could   every   many   most   their   would

Use them to complete the words below.

__ a __ __   w __ __ __ __   a __ __ e __

__ __ e i __   c __ u __ __   e __ e __ __

__ e __ a u __ __   __ o __ __

B Draw lines to show where the syllables split in these words.

albatross   killer   wandering   thousands   morning

soaring   following   flashing   thinking   surging   towards

8 Things under the sea

1 What do you know about sea creatures?

A Write **four** questions about sea creatures that you would like to find the answers to.

Don't forget to add the question mark (?).

1 _____

2 _____

3 _____

4 _____

B Finish these words using **er**, **ar**, **or**, **our**, or **re**

und_____   cent_____   ov_____   pill_____

col_____   aft_____   act_____   nev_____

2 Finding information

A Use the information to finish writing the labels on the diagram.

> A fish breathes through its gills. Gills are slits in the fish's skin. They are just behind the fish's head.
>
> A fish waves its tail to move through the water. The tail is at the other end from the head.
>
> The fish's skin is covered in scales. They help to protect the fish. Fish have several fins. They use these fins to steer.

B Read the words in the table. They all have a tricky bit for spelling.

Write the word and circle the tricky bit. How will you remember it?

Write the word twice more.

word	tricky bit	word	word
every	ev(ery)	every	every
because			
most			
could			
pretty			
sure			
after			
many			
their			
would			

3 Using a glossary

A The alphabet has been written **four** times. Each time, there are some gaps. Can you fill them in?

1 a b __ d e __ g h __ j k __ m __ o __ q __ __ __ u v w x y z

2 __ b __ d __ f __ h __ j __ l __ n __ p __ r __ t __ v __ x y z

3 a __ c d __ f __ __ i __ k l __ n __ __ q r __ t __ v __ x __ z

4 a __ c d __ f __ h i j k __ __ __ o p q __ s __ u v __ x y __

B Choose from one of the words shown to fill in the gaps.

1 There is a nice, ripe _____ (pear/pair) on the tree.

2 She has a new _____ (pear/pair) of shoes.

3 _____ (Dear/Deer) Sunil, Thank you for my gift. It was very kind of you. From Vikash.

4 They saw big _____ (dear/deer) in the forest.

5 "Please come _____," (hear/here) said the teacher.

6 Dad cannot _____ (hear/here) the TV.

4 Writing longer sentences

A Write a joining word to join these pairs of sentences. Choose from *and, because, but, so* or *or*.

1 Fish move well in the water _____ they do not move well on land.

2 Fish have bones _____ people have bones.

3 Saltwater fish cannot live in rivers _____ rivers are fresh water.

4 Freshwater fish can live in rivers _____ they can live in lakes.

5 Fish need fins _____ they can stay the right way up.

B Write the alphabet in your best handwriting. Copy it from the top of page 92.

_____

_____

_____

Now write it again. Can you improve on last time?

_____

_____

_____

5 Summarising information from a text

A Read the longer text about animals that eat fish.

Which animals eat fish?

Fish are eaten by other fish, by birds and also by animals that live on land but hunt in water. They are also eaten by people.

Animals that live on land

Freshwater fish are eaten by grizzly bears. Grizzly bears stand in rivers and catch the racing fish as they swim and leap.

Polar bears eat saltwater fish. They dive deep into the ocean to catch their fish.

Seals and sea lions eat a lot of fish because they are big animals. They spend most of each day hunting.

Other fish

In the ocean, big fish usually eat little fish. The Great White Shark will eat around 250 kg (that is 500 lbs or over 35 stone) of fish each day. That's the same weight as three grown-up people!

Fish that live in shallow water may eat shrimps, crabs and some plants, but most fish eat smaller fish. If a small fish lands on a jellyfish's tentacles, then the jellyfish will eat it.

Birds

Birds eat freshwater and saltwater fish. Ducks and swans live near freshwater and eat freshwater fish, but penguins and pelicans live near saltwater and eat the fish nearby.

Penguins dive deep into the water to hunt for fish. Other birds just dip their heads under the surface to catch their food.

B Underline the most important information in each paragraph. Cross out the information you don't need.

- Finish this summary of the text. Write one or two sentences about each paragraph following the examples.

Summary

Fish are eaten by animals, birds, other fish and people.
Grizzly bears catch fish in rivers but polar bears have to dive into the ocean.
Big animals like seals and sea lions need to eat lots of fish.

_____

_____

_____

_____

_____

6 Summarising information from a chart

A Read the chart on page 96.

Write the most interesting thing you found out.

_____

_____

_____

Sea creatures	What kind of animal is it?	What does it eat?	How does it move?	Interesting fact
Great White shark	Fish	Any animal in the sea	Swims with its fins and its tail	The shark will drown if it stops swimming.
Killer whale	Mammal	Any animal in the sea	Swims with its flippers and its tail	Killer whales are more like dolphins than sharks.
Leatherback turtle	Reptile	Jellyfish	Flaps its flippers in the water. Drags itself on land.	Leatherbacks can grow over 2 m (6 feet) long.
Blue crab	Crustacean	Snails, worms and seaweed	On land it scuttles sideways on ten legs. In water it swims using its legs.	People love eating blue crabs.

B Fill in the gaps in the text using information from the chart.

The Great White shark is a _____ . It moves quickly

through the water and swims using _____ .

Unlike the shark, the killer whale is a _____ . It swims

with its _____ instead of fins.

The _____ is a reptile. It has flippers

too. It swims very well in water but has to _____ itself

on land. It eats _____ . Crabs are _____ .

They eat _____ . They have

_____ legs and they _____ on land.

Unit 8 Things under the sea

7 Looking at tense

A Write the present tense of these verbs in the table.

Use the words you wrote in the table to fill in the gaps below. One is done for you.

Past tense	Present tense
were	are
was	
had	
lived	
ate	
looked	
hunted	

Killer whales ____are____ in the same family as dolphins. They _____ long bodies with black and white marks. Killer whales _____ also called orcas. Orcas _____ fish, squid and other sea animals.

Orcas _____ in groups which are called pods. Orcas in the same pod sometimes _____ together. Pods have between five and 30 orcas in them. The most important orca in a pod _____ a mother.

Baby orcas _____ called calves. The mother _____ after her calf until it _____ about two years old.

B Which six of these words can you add the suffix **ly** to? Write the words on the lines.

real   sit   sad   slow   laugh   beautiful   nice   neat

If the word doesn't make sense to you, don't write it.

_____

_____

8 Finding information on a screen

A Re-read the text about coral reefs. Underline all the words with more than one syllable.

> ### Where are coral reefs?
> Coral reefs grow in seas and oceans which are warm and sunny all year round.
>
> ### What do coral reefs need to grow?
> The water must be clear, calm and peaceful so sunlight can reach the corals and they are not disturbed.
>
> ### Where is the biggest coral reef in the world?
> The biggest coral reef in the world is near Australia. It is called the Great Barrier Reef. It stretches for more than 2600 kilometres (1600 miles).

Write all the words you find tricky to read in this box.

Then:

- cross out the words you can work out by finding the syllables
- cross out the words you can read by working out what you know and guessing the tricky bits.

Write out the words you still find tricky:

- How will you remember them?

Unit 8 Things under the sea

B Make these words into describing words by adding **ful**.

use   power   wonder   care

<u>useful</u>   _____   _____   _____

Write a sentence for each word you wrote.

1 _____

2 _____

3 _____

4 _____

9 Reading report texts

A Choose words from the box to fill the gaps.

| want | helps | live |
| grow | need | feed |

Which fish live in coral reefs?

Many of the world's most colourful fish _____ amongst the corals in a reef. Some fish travel in huge schools of the same fish. This _____ keep them safe from predators who _____ to eat them.

Parrotfish

Parrotfishes' teeth _____ to look like a parrot's beak. Parrotfish _____ tough teeth because they _____ on the hard coral shells that make up the reef.

B Tick (✓) the sentences you would use in a non-chronological report text about reef sharks.

☐ I love reef sharks.

☐ Reef sharks are predators and they eat other fish.

☐ They also hunt crabs, squid, lobsters and shrimp.

☐ Mario saw a reef shark when he was on holiday in India.

☐ Reef sharks are so sweet – they the prettiest of all the sharks.

☐ Reef sharks like shallower water and are often near the surface.

☐ Diver Dan saw a reef shark. He tried to give it sandwiches to eat.

☐ Reef sharks will attack divers if they think the divers are threatening them.

10 Planning a report text

A Sort the facts below into two groups which are about the same thing. Underline each group in a different colour.

Jellyfish

Jellyfish have long tentacles.

Jellyfish float in the sea.

Jellyfish have soft bodies.

Their tentacles are poisonous.

Venom pumps through the tentacles and stings fish.

Most of a jellyfish is made up of water.

Stung fish are taken to the mouth by the oral arms.

B Look at the word p<u>oi</u>son. The underlined sound is written **oi** here, but the same sound is written **oy** in some other words. Write **oi** or **oy** to complete these words.

b __ __   b __ __ l   c __ __ n

enj __ __   t __ __   ch __ __ ce

n __ __ se   ann __ __   p __ __ nt

r __ __ al   sp __ __ l   j __ __ n

11 Writing a report text

A Use the jellyfish facts (on page 100) to write **two** paragraphs of text about jellyfish.

Don't forget to use headings.

_____
_____
_____
_____
_____
_____
_____

B Add five full stops and five capital letters to this text.

sea snails live on and near coral reefs they are more colourful than land snails most of the soft body is hidden in the shell some sea snails eat seaweed but others eat other coral reef creatures they drill holes in the shells of sea clams and suck out the soft body

12 Improving a report text

A Number the sea creatures (1 to 6) in their alphabetical order.

sponge   octopus

jellyfish   anemone

parrotfish   coral

Rewrite the list, putting the creatures in alphabetical order.

a b c d e f g h i j k l m n o p q r s t u v w x y z

1 _____   2 _____   3 _____

4 _____   5 _____   6 _____

B Choose three of the creatures. Write a sentence about each creature for a glossary to tell people something about it.

_____

_____

_____

_____

_____

_____

Unit 8 Things under the sea

Unit review

A Read the list of words. Write them in the box that shows the **sound** of the vowel. It is underlined each time.

b<u>ea</u>r   b<u>ea</u>rd   col<u>our</u>   d<u>are</u>   d<u>eer</u>

gr<u>ou</u>nd   j<u>oi</u>n   s<u>ou</u>nd   t<u>oy</u>   ov<u>er</u>

oi	ow	ear	air	er
boil	cow	hear	chair	butter

B All of these words have the letter **a**. Read the words aloud.

apple   any   alone   apron   father   angle

swan   about   half   what   many   April

1 How many different ways can you find of saying the letter sound?

_____

2 Write the words in pairs where the letter **a** has the same sound.

9 All kinds of creatures

1 Looking at jokes

A Read the jokes.

Underline the words or sounds that make the joke funny.

1. Why do bees hum? Because they don't know the words.

2. Why did the man throw the butter out the window? Because he wanted to see butterfly.

3. Why does everyone love cats? Because they're purr-fect.

4. What do you call a fly without wings? A walk.

5. Where do cows go with their friends? The moooovies!

6. Which fish only swims at night? Starfish

7. What do you call a bear with no ear? A 'b'

B Which joke did you like best? Copy it out below using your best handwriting.

Tip

Look at the sizes of the letters in the alphabet. Which letters are tall? Which letters have long tails? Which letters are the same height as each other? Try to make your letters the same sizes as these.

a b c d e f g h i j k l m n o p q r s t u v w x y z

_____

_____

_____

C Write the missing word in each line. It sounds like the word in the box, but it is spelled differently.

Sounds like	Write the missing word.
bee	She should _____ in school today.
two	Are you going _____ school _____?
there	They hung up _____ bags.
hear	Are you planning to stay _____?
wear	_____ are you going?

2 Poems about cats

A Read this poem. Write rhyming words on the empty lines.

The Apple and the Worm

I bit an apple
    That had a worm.
I swallowed the apple,
    I swallowed the w_____ .
I felt it squiggle
    I felt it squirm.
I felt it wiggle,
    I felt it t_____ .
I felt it so slippery,
    Slimy, scummy,
I felt it land – PLOP –
    In my t_____ !
I guess that worm is
    there to stay
Unless …
I swallow a bird some d_____ !

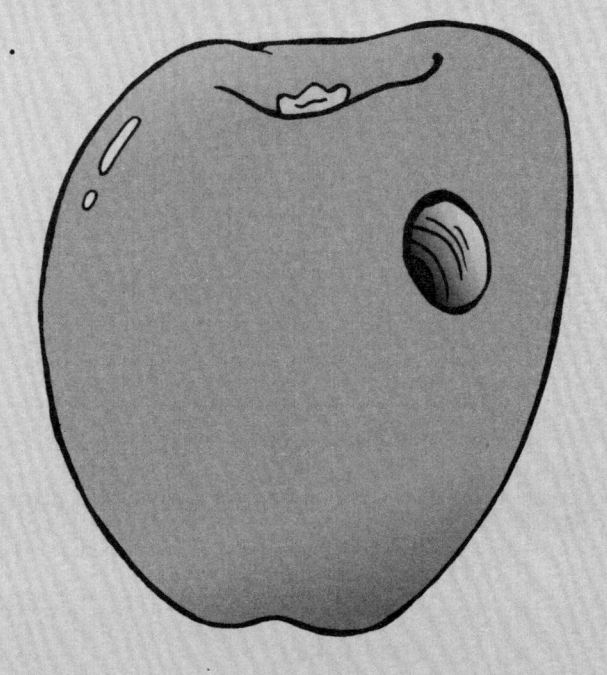

Robert Heidbreder

B Draw the picture that the poem makes in your head.

Unit 9 All kinds of creatures

3 Reading aloud

A Answer the questions about *The Apple and the Worm*.

1 Tick (✓) what the poet ate.

☐ an apple ☐ an apple and a worm

☐ a worm ☐ an orange

2 How did the poet know that he had eaten the worm? Give one example.

_____

3 Write *two* words the poet used to describe the worm.

_____

4 How does the poet think he might get rid of the worm?

_____

5 How do you think the poet was feeling after he had eaten the apple?

_____

B Ask someone to time you reading the words in the box below. How many can you read in one minute? _____

Underline any that you had to 'pass' on, then practise them.

don't	old	by	house	about	your	here	saw
said	there	want	where	who	why	which	what
put	very	people	called	asked	could	their
most	every	pretty	sure	after	because	many

4 Learn and recite

A Complete the words using the sounds given.

sounds like <u>oi</u>l	sounds like r<u>ou</u>nd	sounds like n<u>ear</u>	sounds like h<u>air</u>
oi, oy	ow, ou	ear, eer, ere	air, are, ear
c _____ n	_____ l	cl _____	ch _____
j _____	_____ t	d _____	c _____
j _____ n	cl _____ n	d _____	d _____
b _____	cl _____ d	h _____	w _____
b _____ l	fl _____ er	h _____	sh _____
	gr _____ nd	b _____ d	

5 Plan a poem

A Read this poem. Draw lines to join words that rhyme.

Little Jack Horner

Little Jack Horner

Sat in the corner

Eating a big, fruit pie.

He put in his thumb

And pulled out a plum,

And said, "What a good boy am I!"

Unit 9 All kinds of creatures

B Write your own version of the poem.

Try your ideas out here:

Little _____

Sat _____

Eating _____

He _____

And _____

And _____

6 Publishing a poem

A Re-read your version of *Little Jack Horner*.
Are there any spelling mistakes? Correct any words.

B Copy your poem in your best handwriting.

_____

_____

_____

_____

Unit review

A Write as many words as you can that rhyme with:

pound	
coil	
flare	
deer	

B Read these pairs of lines.

Twinkle twinkle little star.
Do you have a brand new car?

Twinkle twinkle little dog.
You must not chase the bright green frog!

Add your own second line to these opening lines:

Twinkle twinkle little shoe.

_____

Twinkle twinkle little light.

_____

Unit 9 All kinds of creatures

C What do you have to remember when you are writing poetry? Write one thing in each space.

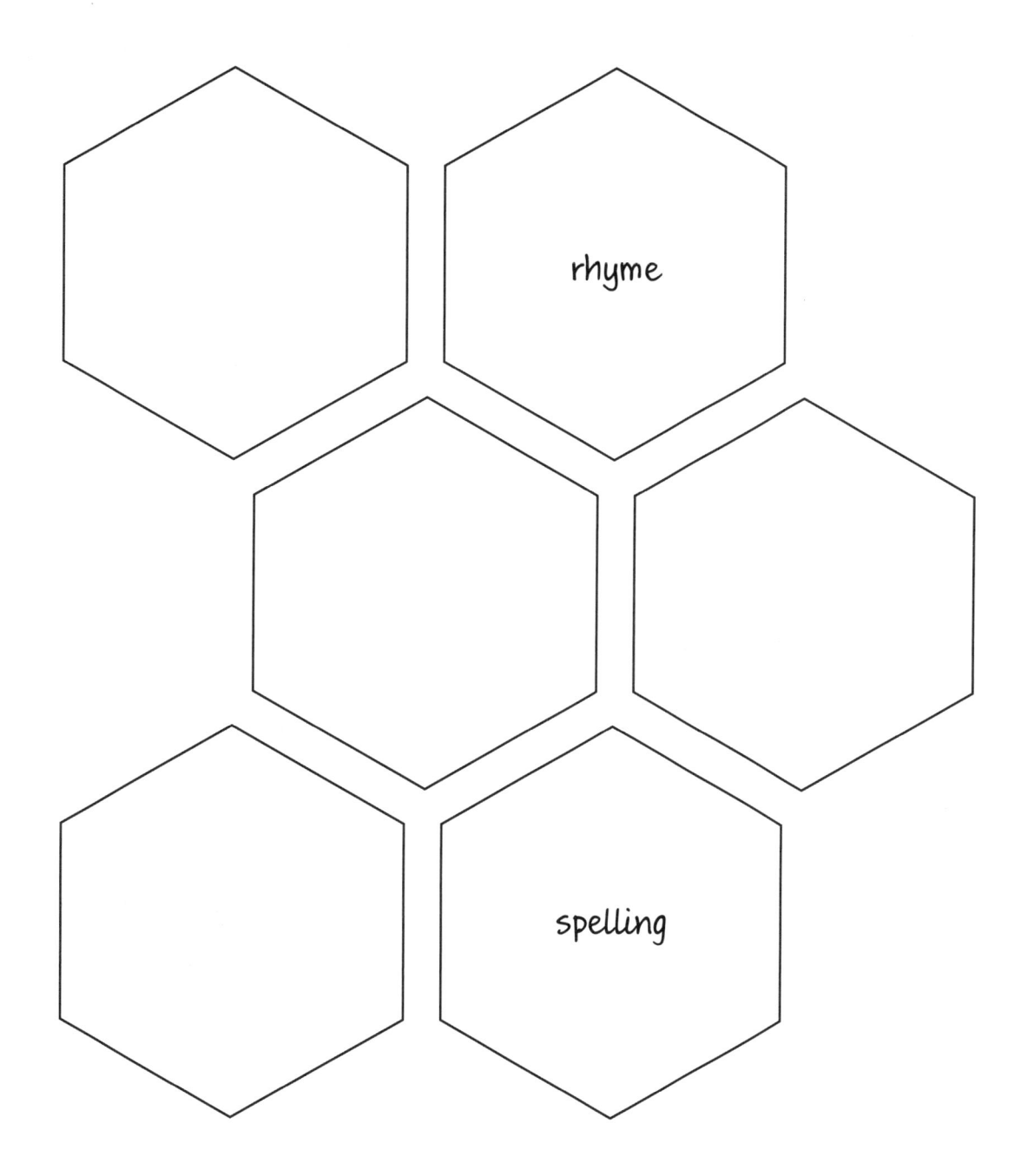

rhyme

spelling

Acknowledgements

The authors and publishers acknowledge the following sources of copyright material and are grateful for the permissions granted. While every effort has been made, it has not always been possible to identify the sources of all the material used, or to trace all copyright holders. If any omissions are brought to our notice, we will be happy to include the appropriate acknowledgements on reprinting.

p. 5 Text © 1988 Dick King-Smith from Sophie's Snail by Dick King-Smith, reproduced by permission of Walker Books Ltd, London SE11 5HJ www.walker.co.uk illustrations not from original publication; p. 7 'The Things Mums Say' by Michaela Morgan, used by permission of the author; p. 13 text and illustrations from BUNNY MONEY by Rosemary Wells, copyright © 1997 by Rosemary Wells. Used by permission of Viking Children's Books, a division of Penguin Young Readers Group, a member of Penguin Group (USA) LLC; p. 31 'Younger Brother' copyright © Trevor Millum, first published in Too Much Shopping Can Damage Your Health, EJ Arnold, 1997; pp. 38, 39 extracts from How the Bear Lost His Tail by Susan Price, illustrated by Sara Ogilvie (OUP, 2011), text copyright © Susan Price 2011, illustrations copyright © Sara Ogilvie 2011, reprinted by permission of Oxford University Press; p. 45 Extracts from Yoshi the Stonecutter by Becca Heddle (OUP 2011), text copyright © Becca Heddle 2011, reprinted by permission of Oxford University Press; p. 68 'Busy Day' by Michael Rosen, from A Book of Very Silly Poems by Michael Rosen, Puffin Books, 1997. Reproduced by permission of Penguin Books Ltd; p. 71 'Downhill Racer' by Roger McGough from All the Best: the selected poems of Roger McGough (Puffin Books, 2004) by permission of United Agents; p. 72 'The River' by Valerie Bloom in One River, Many Creeks by Valerie Bloom, by permission of Eddison Pearson Ltd; p. 76 excerpt from The Hodgeheg by Dick King-Smith, Puffin Books, 1989. Reproduced by permission of Penguin Books Ltd and AP Watt at United Agents; p. 79 excerpt from The Lost Happy Endings by Carol Ann Duffy, illustrated by Jane Ray, © Carol Ann Duffy, 2008, Bloomsbury Publishing Plc; p. 73 'The Sea' by James Reeves, reproduced by permission of the Laura Cecil Literary Agency; p. 106 'The Apple and the Worm' by Robert Heidbreder, published by Fitzhenry & Whiteside, Canada

Cover artwork: Bill Bolton

The publisher is grateful to the following expert reviewers: Lois Hopkins, Mary Millet, Iram Mohsin, Geeta Prakash.

Photographs

p20 © andresrimaging / iStock / ThinkStock; p37 *t* © Gert Vrey / Shutterstock, *b* © VladyslavDanilin / iStock / ThinkStock; p40 *t-b* © edella / iStock / ThinkStock, © johan10 / iStock / ThinkStock, © GlobalP / iStock / ThinkStock, © IvanMikhaylov / iStock / ThinkStock, © rob_lan / iStock / ThinkStock, © NK08gerd / iStock / ThinkStock; pp60 and 61 *t-b* © sokolkz / iStock / ThinkStock, © Edward Westmacott / iStock / ThinkStock, © Andreas Weber / iStock / ThinkStock; p64 *t* © Waltraud Ingerl / iStock / ThinkStock, *b* © Medioimages/Photodisc / Getty Images; p65 © paulcutler62 / iStock / ThinkStock; p69 © Odua Images / Shutterstock; p71 © Jupiterimages / Stockbyte / Getty Images; p75 *t r-l* © Andreka / iStock / ThinkStock, © fotorince / iStock / ThinkStock, © LuminaStock / iStock / ThinkStock, © Hemera Technologies / PhotoObjects.net / Thinkstock, *c l-r* © g-stockstudio / iStock / ThinkStock, © miflippo / iStock / ThinkStock, © seread / iStock / ThinkStock, © HonBK1988 / iStock / ThinkStock, *b l-r* © Ingram Publishing / Getty Images, © Medioimages/Photodisc / Getty Images, © ajlber / iStock / ThinkStock, © rasikabendre / iStock / ThinkStock; p94 *t-b* © Michal_K / Shutterstock, © Joe Belanger / Shutterstock, © Uvimages / amanaimagesRF /ThinkStock; p99 © Michael Stubblefield / iStock / ThinkStock; p100 © Michael Stubblefield / iStock / ThinkStock; p102 © Boris Pamikov / Shutterstock

Key: *t* = top, *c* = centre, *b* = bottom, *l* = left, *r* = right.